THROUGH TRANSPORT SECURITY
a practical guide

British Library Cataloguing in Publication Data
Elliott, Paul
    Through transport security
    1. Cargoes. Thefts. Security measures
    I. Title
    388.0440687

    ISBN 1-85609-011-6

THROUGH TRANSPORT SECURITY
a practical guide

PAUL ELLIOTT

A Witherby Practical Guide

LONDON

WITHERBY & CO. LTD.

32-36 Aylesbury Street,
London EC1R 0ET
Telephone 071-251 5341
Fax No. 071-251 1296

First Published 1990

© Paul Elliott 1990

ISBN 1 85609 011 6

AUTHORS PREFACE

It was my specific intention not to write this book in the form of a rigid manual of procedure. Instead I have set out to present a readable appraisal of the subject and above all to guide through transport organisations, their customers and their insurers towards a thoroughly commercial policy of sensible precautions against common losses within the industry. The contents will also be useful to lawyers who may be asked to judge what is fair and reasonable in terms of security precaution. The assumption is justifiably made that both organised and opportunist crime will occur if not deterred in an era when police resources do not stretch to dealing with the majority of it and private security companies are self regulated in an unsatisfactory manner. In any case, security is a preventative science and is achieved by sound procedure and defence. Above all, in an industry which is about the careful handling of others' property, security can be shown as a contribution to the bottom line of the balance sheet and to be a marketing tool. When security goes wrong, those responsible can be held to be accountable and an effective recovery can be made.

The security function in industry and commerce as a whole, is largely motivated by self preservation. However, the recently formulated maritime security legislation in the UK and anti-drug trafficking agreement promoted by the USA and New Zealand have created a new dimension for security at sea ports and in shipping companies. I have attempted to interpret these regulations into sensible commercial practise.

ABOUT THE AUTHOR

Paul Elliott is a Fellow of the International Institute of Security. He served for over twenty years with the Royal Air Force, leaving as a commissioned officer in the Security and Provost Branch. He had specialised in security survey and investigations working latterly in air transport security operations before a final appointment with the Ministry of Defence in London. Paul's commercial career started when he joined Burmah-Castrol Oil as Chief Security Officer. Since 1987 he has been Security Adviser to the P & O Containers group of companies. Through his work on several security committees of the British Standards Institute he was appointed Chairman of a new committee charged with writing a user standard for security seals. He is also a member of the International Institute of Security examination question panel and a member of the International Association of Airport and Seaport Police.

ACKNOWLEDGEMENTS

We are most appreciative of material supplied by Headlight Magazine (Plate 1) also to Photoscan Limited (Plates 2, 6 and 7)

TYPICAL THROUGH TRANSPORT CHAIN

Diag. 1

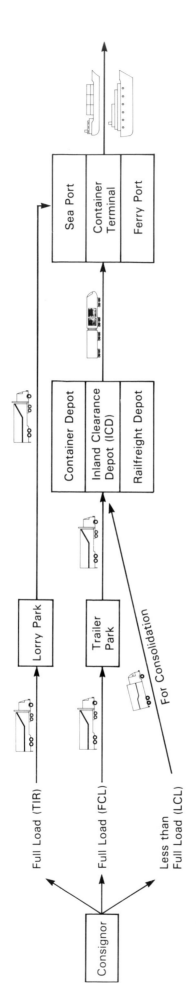
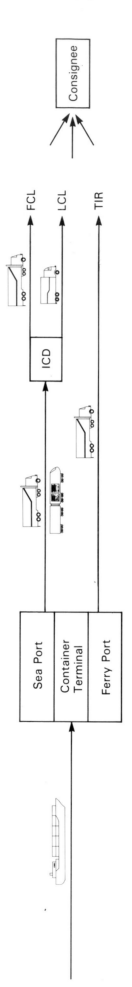

CONTENTS

Chapter 1

Through Transport Security Risks

THROUGH TRANSPORT SECURITY RISKS

The risks of a through transport operation which beg the application of security practise can be represented in two main areas, loss of profit and loss of reputation. The latter is paramount in a competitive commercial environment which is all about the protection of property in transit, in the form of cargo, belonging to another. Reputation can be enhanced by security at the marketing presentation stage and also in the recovery stage which inevitably follows any loss i.e. quick and professional investigation response, which can also lead to useful education of the customer in the form of gratuitous consultancy. An open and responsible attitude in these circumstances can often turn a disaster into a victory in business relationships with customers.

The security risks that can lead to loss of profits are as follows, some less obvious than others:

(a)   Theft/Substitution and Damage/Contamination — both of cargo and of equipment.

(b)   Loss of commercial information

(c)   Fraud

(d)   Drug Trafficking — through penalties imposed by customs authorities.

(e)   Import control failures — through fines imposed by customs and excise authorities.

(f)   Legislative Breaches — through fines imposed by governments.

(g)   Insurance Losses — resulting from both failure to make recovery and payment of enhanced premiums.

The ensueing chapters of this book cover the methods by which these risks can be addressed in a balanced, practical manner. However, we should first put some of these risks into perspective and quantify them in both financial and commercial terms.

Theft of Cargo

This falls into two categories, the loss of the complete load and pilferage (the loss of part of the load). The latter is clearly less of an immediate financial burden but it can often be regarded as more of a penalty in nuisance terms by the customer. At the time of writing, in 1990, total loss high risk cargo values can be exemplified as follows:

(a)   Container load (40ft.) of dutiable cigarettes: £850,000

(b)   Container load (40ft.) of finished electronic products: £50,000 — £500,000

There are also "special" loads such as bullion where a 20ft. box may be worth over £2m. Whilst in limited liability terms, the financial loss to the carrier may be much less than these figures, it is not unknown for commercial pressure from the customer to result in full value settlements. Even when liability cannot be satisfactorily proved against the carrier, ex gratia settlements may be judged to be a preferred option to loss of future business. There has been recent relevant case law on limits of liability related to poor security; in TEXAS INSTRUMENTS LTD AND ANOTHER v EUROPE CARGO LTD AND OTHERS Queens Bench Division: Mr Justice Tudor Evans: 29 June 1990. The case involved the theft of an articulated trailer load of machine instruments. The carrier instructed his driver to deliver the trailer to an insecure park in London where he was to leave it for collection by another driver some while later. The first driver pointed out to his employer (the carrier) that security of he load was not adequate unless taken to a secure site but his advice was not heded and the load was in fact stolen. The carrier was sued for the full value of the load but he claimed limited liability under the CMR Convention enacted in the Carriage of Goods by Road Act 1965. Had the carrier ensured reasonable security of the load, then his liability would have been limited but, because he ignored advice to the effect that security was inadequate, he was judged to have been negligent (the damage being caused by his wilful misconduct) and therefore a claim for the full value of the cargo was in order. Far better then, to invest in security measures which reduce the risk of attack by thieves, also to promote an incentive to care for all agents and contractors by implementing security audit which will ensure that responsibility for loss is clearly attributed.

Drug Trafficking Penalities

These penalties, imposed on cargo carriers by customs authorities can make losses by theft pale into insignificance. They can result in confiscation of the carrying vessel or multi-million dollar fines, typical United States Customs penalty scales for 1989 were US$1000 per ounce for herion and cocaine, and US$500 per ounce for marijuana and derivatives found concealed in cargo consignments or on board a ship or aircraft.

It is the authors' opinion that, because organised drug trafficking of large consignments involves the covert use of normal commercial freight channels, it is not a question of "if" but one of "when" a carrier of international cargo will experience the imposition of these penalties. However, through international customs co-operation, there is a growing popularity for what the United States call Carrier Initiative Programs. Carriers can register their agreement to implement a number of actions as recommended by the customs, these are principally physical security measures on vessels and in ports. The idea is that such implementation, if it can be proven, will significantly mitigate the case against the carrier should he be penalised under anti-drug legislation. In these circumstances, the penalty is set in line with the appropriate scale and then the carrier has 30 days to present his case in mitigation. If this is satisfactory (it is no good promosing to implement measures in the future, you have to show established practice retrospectively) then the carrier may be deemed to have exercised "maximum care and diligence" with the result that the penalty will be radically reduced or even waived altogether.

Most of the measures stipulated by these agreements are sound preventative actions which are consistent with those that a diligent company will enforce in the normal course of business. Some however, are more specialist and there is some justifiable concern that customs may take unfair advantage of the moral issues at stake, to persuade private companies to carry out work which is not rightfully their responsibility. This refers principally to intelligence gathering, beyond the obligation to pass on information which is gratuitously received in the course of business, and investigation and search of individuals, when the legal requirements cannot be fulfilled. Further mention of these areas will be made later, mainly in chapters 4 and 5.

Maritime Security Legislation

In 1982, the UK government enacted legislation which requires airlines and airport operations to implement anti-terrorist security measures. At the time of writing, this legislation is being up-dated and extended to include the maritime industry. The requirements will apply to the owners of all vessels calling at British ports, regardless of flag, and to port owners including any company operating within a port. In order to assess the effect this will have on the industry, one can recall the experience of the aviation world and see that whilst airlines had to comply, they relied heavily on the security facilities provided for them on the ground at airports. The same will happen in shipping. There will however be a considerable difference in the initial effort required at seaports. Airports were already somewhat secure. They had perimeter fencing (mainly to prevent the public and animals straying on to the active runways) and the operational buildings were segregated for both customs and immigration purposes; the airside/landside principal had long been established. Sea ports are largely devoid of these fundamental controls. The legislation, aimed to dilute the terrorist threat, talks of enforcement scaled to the imminence of such an attack and it is true that some measures will be possible to implement at short notice. However, they will have to be built on fundamental physical security facilities such as fences, gates, control points and intruder detection systems which must be installed on a contingency basis. Also it is not possible to deploy large forces of security officers overnight, despite claims of some guarding contractors. This may all seem commercially daunting but, in fact, the chapters of this book will seek to show that such continuous measures can contribute positively in a loss prevention role, and so are not unrealistic. It is also worth mentioning that aviation terrorism is principally targetted at passengers and the maritime legislation will initially be concentrated on cruising and ferry operations. Through transport industry readers may therefore be forgiven for questionning how all this affects them. The reasons can be listed as follows:

(a)   On a worldwide scale, acts of terrorism against cargo shipping are increasing, particularly in terms of economic targetting.

(b)   Terrorist interference with cargo represents a threat to ferries carrying both passengers and freight.

(c)   Terrorist interference with hazardous cargo could threaten the environmental safety of a seaport or coastal town.

(d)   There will be a physical terrorist threat to the channel tunnel and it is likely that security legislation will be extended to cover anti-explosive screening of rail freight; for example, containers in the through transport system.

Penalties for non-compliance with this type of legislation are likely to be similar to those imposed under health and safety laws. The significant threat to a business will be that of a prohibition notice which could interrupt business until "the fences are mended" — a lengthy and expensive situation if security has not been a planning consideration and totally integrated with the core operation.

Illus·1   TIR Tautliner

Chapter 2

Responsibility for Security

RESPONSIBILITY FOR SECURITY

Corporate Responsibility

There can be no argument that security is a fundamental component of any through transport operation. Part of the package offered by the carrier's salesman to his customer is the care that will be exercised in delivering the cargo safely and soundly. Operational staff are actually practising security as they go about moving and storing the cargo so that although the ultimate responsibility for security may be that of the Managing Director, there is full and thorough delegation of that responsibility down to the line management at each stage of the through transport chain. It is of course right, in any efficient company, that line management should be fully accountable for their part of the operation, including its security. However, because the standards of security must be constantly maintained in this industry, there is also a need for professional audit and for qualified advice on the security systems and procedures employed. This necessitates the recruitment of specialist security personnel.

Employment of Security Staff

Most of the security staff employed in the industry are supplied under contract by security guarding companies. These contracts require enormous care in their commissioning followed by continual supervision and it is for this reason that we will be subjecting them to detailed examination in due course. It is also the reason why the industry needs to directly employ professional security managers, some in a centralised (corporate) role and one, say, at each major interchange location e.g. large container depot or seaport facility.

These line security managers will have a day to day control over contract staff whilst those in a corporate role will be highly experienced in all aspects such as physical and electronic security systems, security and criminal investigation, specification and montoring of security contracts and also the specialist areas of transportation security. In short, they will carry out a security policy development role and internal audit.

It is important to recognise that there is no substitute for these people who will usually have a background in formal security (such as that obtained in government service) or, possibly from the police. We should mention The Police Force at this stage on two counts. Firstly, they should in no way be regarded as gratuitous support for industry. They are a reactive force who have limited capacity and whose response is usually concentrated on much more serious crimes than routine theft. Secondly, they have little pro-active experience; crime prevention officers run a domestic service and have insufficient experience to offer security advice to industrial concerns.

There are some private police forces who operate within the environments used by the through transport industry. The British Transport Police operate in conjunction with the railways but again they are a mainly reactive organisation. There are dock police forces too, such as the Port of London Authority Police who used to protect the vast area of the London Docks but now are quite a small force operating mainly at Tilbury. The fact of the matter is that whilst these isolated forces have police powers, that is, the legal power to arrest, detain and search and the deterrent appearance signified by their uniform, they are extremely expensive when compared to civilian security organisations and, in economic terms alone, their future must be very uncertain.

Guarding Contractors

There is much to consider here which is common to the employment of security guarding services anywhere. Guarding contractors have been much maligned publicy for their lack of standards but this is as much to do with the lack of recognition by their clients of the controls which they need to exercise, as it is to do with the self regulating aspects of the service sector. The bald fact is that, whilst these contractors seek to offer a specialist security service, they draw their operational employees from a relatively unqualified pool of the labour market. They can be likened in many ways to the other services such as cleaners, messengers and caterers but there is one significant difference. All these others can have their performance easily and continually measured; if your office waste bin has not been emptied then you know immediately that the cleaner has failed, but because the guard is there largely for a contingency event (a visit by thieves or vandals) which does not happen every day, you do not know if he is being constantly efficient. It is a sad fact that the guarding industry knows this and the unscrupulous (ranging from a totally fraudulent company to the cost centre manager of a good company who seeks to improve his profit margin by sharp practise) do take advantage. Examples of poor standard produced by guarding contractors include:

1.   Inadequate vetting of recruits

2.   Very high turnover of staff

3.   Very poor pay

4.   Excessive working hours (over the industry standard of 60 per week)

5.   Poor levels of training

6.   Deliberate failure to complete all contracted hours.

The client must recognise all of these (and more) and negotiate a contract which negates them. We shall be looking at the specific uses of security guards within the through transport industry in Chapter 5 so suffice to say here that it is the client who must specify his own security policy and procedures and instruct the contractor to work to these; it is safest to assume that security guarding contractors have no specialist security knowledge (they just supply uniformed personnel who are disciplined by a centralised back up and control system) and then one can be pleasantly surprised if the contrary turns out to be true. Readers might ask at this stage why we consider using these contractors at all, the answer being simply that it is more cost effective to contract out rather than try to administer the 'hot seat' supply of manpower (security guarding is a continuity job where there can be no question of the position being unfilled, even for an hour or two) as an ancilliary to your core business.

Before we move on to the contract itself, there is one golden rule which should, if possible, be followed. There will be clients who envisage the economy of only employing security guards during the 'silent hours', that is say 8pm to 6am or just at weekends from Saturday lunchtime. This formula could well turn out to be a false economy because it does not allow a guarding contractor to employ full time staff who are dedicated to this one contract. It will lead to staff discontinuity (constant re-training), excessive hours being worked, staff fatigue and poor quality guarding. Far better to avoid this temptation and award a 168 hour (per week) contract, that is to say one man continuously or in multiples of this. The guarding industry works a standard 60 hour week, that is 5 x 12 hour shifts per week, and 3 men are required for this cover. They are shift rostered to work 60 hours for each of 2 weeks and 48 hours during the third. Don't worry, we shall talk about guard utilisation in Chapter 5, but the daytime hours can easily be utilised and be very cost effective indeed.

The Contract

All guarding companies will supply a contract document which neatly spells out their standard terms and conditions. It will broadly say that the service is a deterrent only and does not guarantee total security; This is fair as far as it goes because no one could be expected to 'hold on to the money' with a sawn-off shotgun held to his throat.

However, the basic document is rarely adequate on its own, it needs a set of assignment instructions (the detail of the precise security duties required) attached as an annex and also, even given that the client's lawyer is happy with the terms, some clarification of the standards expected. The following is a guide to contractual stipulation which should be demanded of every guarding contractor.

a. Staff vetting
It is well known that UK employers of security staff do not have right of access to criminal records. This does not however excuse them from very careful background checks. Pre-

employment integrity vetting should have been carried out to cover a period of five years prior to application. Within the three months following recruitment, satisfactory references confirming integrity for the whole of the previous twenty years (or from the date of commencing secondary education) must have been obtained by the employer. Medical fitness is also a major consideration, to the degree necessary for the duties within the contract. Additional safeguards which could be required include age limitations (say between 20 and 60) and a provision that guards must have at least two years' proven service previously with the contractor. Clearly, this latter stipulation could not be promised to all clients but, if your security is vital, why not ask for it?

b. Staff Turnover

Security guarding as a job does not suit everyone due to the long and unsocial hours. This can lead to a high turnover of staff particularly in the first four weeks of the contract. Much of this is a failure by the contractor to explain the minus points of a particular assignment to new recruits but he can be persuaded to take greater care over this. One method that some highly discerning clients have used is to include a financial penalty in the contract should staff turnover exceed a particular rate. Perhaps the most sound idea is for the client to take great interest in the particular individuals being selected for the work and perhaps interview them before employment at the assignment. There is also a link with pay.

c. Pay Rates

Pay in the guarding industry can be notoriously poor. At the time of writing (in 1990) UK rates of less than £2. per hour can still be seen for the standard 60 hour working week. Nevertheless, £4. per hour is considered good, even in London. Obviously, some blame for such exploitation must be the effect of market forces, dictated by an extremely competitive situation and some lack of sensible recognition by clients that 'one only gets what one pays for'. It is not true however that to pay a high premium is cost effective either because the nature of the work will only attract satisfactory employees from a relatively small pool.

The answer to this is for the client to establish a clear understanding of both the market and the requirement. It is then perfectly legitimate to stipulate the hourly pay rate at contract tender stage; price quotations are then based on the charge for the service and contractors overheads. A rough guide is that the guards gross pay (excluding Employers National Insurance Contributions) should be around 65% of the contract price. If such an agreement is reached, subsequent increases can be negotiated proportionally and related to the quality of back-up from the contractor and to the performance of the guards. It makes sense to run regular checks to ensure that the pay levels are maintained; some clients request sight of pay slips but, more simply, just ask the guards!

Pay is also linked to the problem of excessive working hours.

d. Working hours

As already mentioned, most guards are expected to work 5 x 12 hour shifts per week. There are some areas of the industry where 8 hour shifts are worked but these are sparse and the market is not yet ready for this although the Continental influence in future years might change things.

The problem really is that 60 hours is enough for anyone to work when this includes night shifts. Hours worked in excess of this are detrimental to security awareness mainly because of fatigue. Unfortunately, there are a number of situations which cause 'overtime' and to which the client must be continally aware. For example:—

    (i)   Demand from guards on low pay — sometimes this is disguised from the clients due to employment of his staff on other clients assignments. This can become very serious especially if guards seek to work consecutive shifts, i.e. 12 hours at night followed immediately by 12 hours on the following day.

    (ii)   Deception by the contractor, e.g. he has proposed a 168 hour week, set up with 3 guards; he actually splits the work between 2 guards thus not only inducing fatigue but also charging for the overhead cost for the third guard. This is unfortunately a common problem, the deliberate element of which is masked by the contractor continually claiming that it is difficult to recruit for the assignment.

(iii) Either your assignment or one of another client requires only part-time cover. Rather than recruit for the part-time assignment, the contractor will use guards who are permanently employed on a full time assignment and who are already completing their full working week there.

The solution to this problem is firstly stipulation in contract and, secondly, regular audit. A typical restraining clause in contract is as follows:—

"No shift should exceed 12 working hours and nor should any security officer work more than 60 hours in any period of 7 days. At no time should an officer be required to work more than one successive shift and, prior to the commencement of his shift, each officer should have been off duty for at least 12 hours."

e. Training
There are two kinds of training for security guards. The first is the basic knowledge which anyone in this capacity should pocess. The second is often overlooked, particularly by the client, and is the special training required for the assignment.

Basic training should be given by the contractor to every guard before he or she is assigned to a client. Confirmation should be obtained that this training includes the following:

(i) Powers and practise of arrest

(ii) Powers and practise of search

(iii) Scenes of crime (mainly preservation of evidence)

(iv) Report writing and incident log maintenance

(v) Custody and issue of keys

(vi) Use of the telephone

(vii) Found/lost property

(viii) Foot patrolling

(ix) Fire precautions

(x) Use of radio communications (if applicable)

(xi) Medical First Aid (if applicable)

Assignment training must be in accordance with guidance given by the client. It should be carried out by the contractor but it is often a good thing for the client to provide instruction also. In general, the sort of subjects may be the operation of security systems on the site or the method of checking client employee identify cards. More specific subjects allied to the through transport industry will be discussed in chapter 5.

Poor training can be a common problem, particularly allied to excessive turnover of staff. It is imperative however, in terms of contractual liability, that trained staff are utilised and that if specialist training is necessary by the client, it is given to all the guards employed on the assignment.

f. Completion of Contracted Hours
It has already been mentioned that one of the advantages of employing a security contractor is that of his logistical ability to cover the assignment continually; should a continuously guarded site be left unattended during the 'silent hours', a very serious weakness in security occurs. Usually it is understood that if a guard fails to report and take over duty at a single manned site, then the off-going guard should remain on overtime until he is relieved. This is perhaps the only time when overtime is legitimate in the normal course of events but it must be ensured that such incidents occur very infrequently. However, the real reason that I have included this subject as a problem is that some contractors are known to regularly short man sites, say in the dead of the

night or at a weekend, deliberately in order to save on costs. More often than not it is to practise "ghosting" which is the expression used to describe the covering of two assignments (different clients) which are perhaps geographically close together, using the same manpower.

There is no short cut to a check on this practise but for the client to physically check the guarding presence on a random basis. More about this later because it is the main method of performance monitoring.

Tendering

It is good practise, as with all service contracts, to go out to tender to a number of suppliers. As a recommendation, four such suppliers is usually enough.

The first action is to write the specification for the assignment which should include some precise detail as follows:

(a) A description of the site and its business

(b) The general duties required of the security staff.

(c) How many staff are envisaged.

(d) Any contractual conditions which will be applied.

The next action is to compile the tender list. One of the advantages of employing a good security manager is that he will know contractors of repute. Nevertheless there are some good common sense rules of thumb which can be applied:—

(a) The contractor should be a registered company; big is not always beautiful but the tender list should have a mix of household names and smaller local companies.

(b) The contractor must have a base (or control centre) locally, say within 5 miles of the site. This is important when it comes to operational response.

(c) If you have a multi-site operation in various locations, then you may wish to select contractors who can serve all of them but, again, this is not always a good thing because a mix can be an incentive for each to compete by performance for the chance of your 'group contract' at some later date.

(d) References from other clients of security contractors in your area can be sought.

When it is time to invite proposals, is it a very good idea to hold a single briefing day when all the contractors on the tender list may send representatives to see the site and receive the tender specifications together. There are a number of advantages.

(a) You save time in not having to brief each contractor separately.

(b) None of the contractors can claim that another was given a different brief or presented with an advantageous opportunity.

(c) There is a good chance that all the proposals and quotations will be standardised and easy to compare when considered by the tender board.

(d) All the contractors know who else is tendering; this should ensure that their responses are competitive and realistic.

It is usually a good thing to give between 2 and 4 weeks for the tenders to be prepared and state a specific date by which all should be received. Thereafter it is a matter of choice. You may not wish to accept the most expensive quotation or the least, but judge which company is most likely to provide the best service. Incidentally, when comparing prices, do ensure that monthly or annual quotations have calculated bank holiday overtime rates in the same manner, it is often better to state that the quotation should be an hourly rate inclusive of the 8 UK bank holidays. Ultimately this has another advantage in that if your company accounting is centralised, you will not be faced with queries when the monthly invoice varies according to how many bank holidays are included.

Insurance Cover

Apart from Employers' Liability and Public Liability there are a number of other types of insurance cover which a security guarding contractor should have. Some are special to the industry.

(a) **Efficacy and Contractual Liability** insurance extends Public Liability to include damage or loss arising from the failure to carry out the duties prescribed in the contract. This type of insurance is very relevant to the guarding industry.

(b) **Fidelity Guarantee** insurance covers losses resulting from fraud or dishonesty on the part of the guards themselves.

(c) **Loss of Keys** insurance represents a surprisingly common problem in the industry. The client must feel confident that should the keys to his site, or any of the secure areas on his site, be lost while they are in the custody of the guards, then he can immediately take the contingency measure of changing all the relevant locks and that the total cost of the new locks, keys and their installation will be reimbursed by the contractor in due course. 'Consequential Loss following loss of Keys' insurance extends the cover and is vital.

(d) **Wrongful Arrest** cover is also essential. Whilst security guards should be trained in their legal powers, the average citizen is so well aware of his rights these days that it is very easy for wrongful arrest (often developing into assault) to be alleged, and, indeed, committed. The defendant may well be an employee of the client so it is necessary to ensure that the contractor can reimburse the costs of any damages claimed in these circumstances.

It is clearly for the client to ascertain that all the relevant insurance cover is provided by the contractor and, in particular, that the limits of liability are sufficient to provide for the eventualities of each assignment. For example, at a container depot it should be required that the release of a full container by a security guard to a bogus driver be covered by the contractual liability section. At the time of writing (1990) a realistic sum insured for this event would be £1m. per incident.

Supervision of the Contract

Once the contractor has been selected, he usually needs about a month to prepare for taking on the assignment. There is much to do during this period on the part of both the contractor and client. Most important of all is that the assignment instructions are written: these detail all the duties to be performed by the guards and form an annex to the contract. It is best to let the contractor draft the document against his understanding of the remit. It is surprising how many misunderstandings can be identified at this stage and it is a priority for the client to ensure that he is in complete agreement with the final version. By about the 3 week stage the contractor should be able to identify the guards who will be employed and present details of them to the client. This period of a month is also often the period of notice required by an outgoing contractor and in normal circumstances it should be possible to co-ordinate an amicable handover between him and the new encumbant. Do not forget to give him due notice or you could find yourself paying twice for guarding in the first month of the new contract.

As soon as the contract is commissioned, there will be a settling down period of at least a month before a fair judgement of performance can be made. This is the period when training is paramount and staff turnover could occur without notice. The contractor should be routinely adopting a high profile in terms of supervisory/management visits to the assignment and, indeed, whilst this back up function can be allowed to relax as time goes on, there should always be evidence that such visits are regular but at random intervals. It should also be mentioned that a check telephone call system must be set up between the contractor's control centre and the assignment. At a high security container depot, which may be single manned during the 'silent hours', these calls should be hourly to meet both security and safety requirements.

It is also extremely important that the client accepts an audit role as well. Far too many clients put blind faith to the fore and merely let the contractor carry on unchecked. The client therefore should aim to visit the assignment at least once a month on a no-notice basis during the 'silent hours'. Some of these visits will undoubtedly stretch self discipline, but in order to accurately check performance, such visit times as 1am on a weekday morning and 3pm on a Sunday are what is intended. Let us suppose that you are checking a single manned assignment late at night when all round site activity has ceased; here are some pointers as to what to look for:—

1. Approach the site covertly, e.g. car headlights off, and observe from outside. Is the guard alert? Can you see movement within the gatehouse or, perhaps, a CCTV camera panning round to inspect you?

2. Is the site secure e.g. are the gates closed and locked, or can you merely walk on to the site unobserved?

3. Attract the guard's attention and obtain admission to the site. If he does not know you, does he ask for proof of your identity?

4. Once at the guard's work station, observe the scene. Is he smart and alert and is there an efficient atmosphere? Is there evidence of him having the intention to sleep or is he being entertained by a personal television set which would distract him from security system alarm activations?

5. Inspect the site occurence log book. Is there sufficient evidence of telephone check calls and supervisors visits being recorded? Look back to see if the guards have logged on at the beginning of each shift; are they the regular guards or is there a large number of names you have never heard of?

6. Ask the guard to describe a couple of the specific duties he is required to perform. For example, how does he operate the CCTV system or what action would he take if an emergency arises. Also ask him what he thinks of security at the site; this is a most useful question.

Accountability of the Contractor

We have gone into some detail about contract guarding; no excuses for this because it is quite often that the contractor is in sole charge of the clients assets for about two thirds of the year (nights, weekends, Bank holidays)! It is most important that the contractor is made fully accountable. In common law, should a loss occur when the contractor is in charge, it will be for the client to prove negligence. Because the guarding industry sets out to secure against loss, there is no reason why contracts should not be written which reverse this principle; much better for the contractor to have to prove that he protected the property to the very best of his ability, in these circumstances.

Finally, and to exemplify how accountability can be achieved, let us consider a case history.

A client in the haulage industry parked his vehicles overnight in a sprawling site which had once been railway premises. The boundary was delineated by barriers which constituted a perimeter fence although not to high security standards. There were many buildings on site which produced good shadow cover for intruders and on occasions the vehicles had been attacked by vandals. A guarding contractor agreed to position a security officer on site during the 'silent hours'. He would be based in a site office but also carry out regular foot patrols round the site. The vulnerable points, such as the vehicle park, would be visited and the patrol recorded using electronic keys. The guard's data recorder would be downloaded each day to provide a print-out as proof to both contractor and client that the patrols had been completed. All agreed that this procedure would deter intruders but not necessarily prevent them entering the site and doing damage between the patrols which could be observed from a secluded position.

One morning the client's drivers reported for work to find that their vehicles had been broken into and the radios and telephones stolen from the cabs. The client held the guarding contractor liable for the loss and the contract between them required that the contractor should prove that he had not been negligent.

It was found that the guard's data recorder was unserviceable and, although he claimed to have carried out all the patrols, patrol records could not be produced for the night before. Also, print-outs could not be produced for several previous nights showing that the contractor had failed to check audit the patrol records and discover the equipments' unserviceability in reasonable time. The client claimed that the patrols may not have been completed and that the criminals probably took advantage of this lapse. The contractor had no option but to admit negligence and his insurers reimbursed the client for the cost of replacement vehicle radios and telephones in full.

Conclusion

The purchasers of security guarding services must provide their suppliers with an incentive to care but, at the same time, recognise their own operational contribution if the function is to be a success.

Illus·2   Warehouse covered by CCTV

Chapter 3

Container and Load
Compartment Security

CONTAINER AND LOAD COMPARTMENT SECURITY

Containerisation

Most of the cargo which is moved in the through transport mode is packed in containers. In themselves, these steel boxes, either 20 or 40 feet in length, are not sophisticated equipment but they are built to high standards of strength and durability in order to withstand the rigours of handling and hostile environmental conditions. From the security viewpoint, the introduction of containers was seen as a vast improvement over the movement of cargo loose and in bulk. However, whilst both damage and pilferage have been reduced, when it occurs there is often a very long delay in its discovery. Containers are rarely weighed and, if a large proportion of the cargo is pilfered early in its transit, it may prove very difficult to subsequently identify the point of loss simply because one does not view the containers contents at interchange.

There are many stories of containers or vehicle load compartments being physically interferred with to disguise illicit entry. They range from the removal of the door locking mechanism, or even the doors themselves complete with the sealing medium, to making and repairing a hole in the side or the roof. Similar engineering techniques have been used by drug traffickers for slightly different reasons and include more complicated methods such as the construction of false compartments. Obviously such techniques take time and facilities and can be largely obviated by the adoption of environmental security controls such as those described in Chapter 5. In commercial terms there are two types of containerised load. The "Full Container Load" (FCL) is one where the whole of the container is given over to a single shipper and is simply sealed from door to door for the complete transit. The "Less than a Container Load" (LCL) is one where the container is assigned to carry the cargo of more than one shipper and these smaller consignments are consolidated and packed at a container depot. In the destination country, the container is stripped and the cargo distributed loose.

Either way, the method of ensuring integrity of the containerised load is to seal the door locking mechanism using serially numbered security seals.

Security Sealing

The sealing system is of ultimate importance; it represents the legal guarantee of secure transit in the contract between the shipper and the carrier and also is the medium by which the carrier can check the security of the cargo during transit. In simple terms, the original seal affixed to an FCL should be one and the same seal which is finally removed by the consignee. Of course, there are legitimate occasions when a seal may be removed during transit such as for customs or health authority inspection; after this occurs a new seal is fitted and the importance of the seal audit trail is highlighted. This is also the case when using a number of consecutive seals during a multi-drop operation such as is carried out in retail distribution. The seal is broken and a new one fitted at each point of call and the number recorded to ensure cargo integrity between each call.

The importance of security sealing cannot be stressed too much and no excuse is made for a very detailed examination of the subject here and now.

Selection of Seals

The essential quality of a seal which earns the prefix "security" is that it should be indicative of any interference. A seal is not a lock (locks are not suitable in the through transport business because of the impracticability of controlling keys); it's purpose is to indicate continued integrity and immediate evidence of tampering which may have allowed unauthorised access. Therefore, the ultimate property required is that the seal (except electronic types) should only allow removal by destruction and not be capable of re-instatement in a sealed condition following such removal.

The following are some of the qualities which should be common to all seals used for security purposes:

1. **Tamper Resistance** — evidence of unauthorised interference should be readily visible to the normal unaided human eye and undoubtedly confirmed by very simple inspection on handling.

2. **Easy Enplacement** — the seal should be very simple to fit correctly. It should resist the appearance of initial integrity unless positively locked home. Seals often need to be applied by the unknowledgable and correct fitment must be guaranteed if the checking audit process is to be subsequently meaningful. For example, correct fitment of a cable seal, which is closed by one direction pass through the locking mechanism, is not achieved unless the full length of the cable is pulled tight — a significant weakness.

3. **Resistance to 'Murphys' Law** This quality also applies at the fitment stage. Some seals, such as highly indicative dye filled types, can only be guaranteed to work effectively if fitted a particular way up in the vertical plane; when placement is delegated to the unknowledgeable, there is always doubt that it will be done correctly.

4. **Corrosion Resistance** When seals are applied in circumstances where they will be exposed to harsh environmental conditions, they must resist corrosion which either seizes the locking/checking mechanism or denies the clear reading of an identifying code. Examples are either deep sea exposure on the deck of a ship or long term storage of the container in variable weather conditions.

5. **Strength** Seals should be strong enough to resist accidental breakage by routine handling. However there is rarely the need to use very strong seals unless the protected medium is a highly attractive target placed in a ciminally vulnerable area.

6. **Resistance to Counterfeiting** There is no point in fitting a seal with all the qualitites hitherto described if it can be replaced with an easily produced counterfeit; beware plainly manufactured steel bolt or strip seals whose main components can be easily replicated in a basic workshop.

7. **Facility for Unique Coding** It must always be possible, on inspection or removal, to ensure that the seal fitted is the original item. This begs the need for unique coding of each seal, usually in the form of multi number sequence. The code must not be easily removable or changeable. Electronic seals provide this facility by digital readout.

In order to summarise the types of seal most suitable for through transport purposes it is necessary to categorise them broadly.

Strip Seals

First, the light metal or plastic strip seals which are very common. These seals are simple and cheap and, as such, are only suitable for short distance and short timescale uses; the typical multi-drop operation completed over the period of one or two days springs to mind. The main weakness of these seals is that they all break very easily and that most of the metal types corrode to an extent that negates the indicative quality of the locking mechanism. In long distance through transport operations there are often periods of rough handling, for example in the rail freight system, which makes these seals susceptible to accidental breakage. Also harsh environmental conditions such as those experienced by containers stacked on the deck of a deep sea vessel render the metal seals of this type impossibly corroded. The corrosion not only denies correct checking but also can hide earlier tampering with the seal. In summary, these seals are entirely unsuitable for the sealing of through transport containers. They are satisfactory for domestic haulage but even then it is ill advised to use them for sealing attractive or valuable cargoes which are highly pilferable such as electronic products, cigarettes, cosmetics, drugs or wines and spirits. The seal locking aperture provided on tilt cords (used on open top containers and curtain sided vehicles), being quite little, often forces the use of light strip or small gauge cable seals. The latter are marginally better, but in any case, highly attractive cargo should not be transported in soft skinned load compartments.

Illus·3   Seal Types

| Highly indicative bolt seal-the best type for all round through transport use | Light metal strip seal. Good for domestic use but limited suitability in the through transport chain not suitable for containers | Heavy duty bolt seal. Resists simple attack but unnecessary when good environmental security controls are in place. Relatively expensive | Heavy duty cable seal. Main weakness is lack of positive fitment which can allow simple tampering |

Indicative Bolts

This second category is that of the more substantial but highly indicative bolt seals. These are usually made of steel but have plastic components too, which protect from the elements and provide the means of stylised marking. They are usually in two parts which lock together in fitment; this is probably the only disadvantage because they must be issued as a pair and need to be presented together, say in a polythene bag or blister pack. They are medium priced seals but, overall are undoubtedly the best for all round use. The extra cost over strip seals is easily absorbed by the benefits to large through transport operators who can purchase them in bulk and use them universally. This universal standardised use is also a significant cargo theft prevention method because potential thieves are unable to identify valuable cargo by the presence, in isolation, of a more substantial seal.

Heavy Duty Bolts and Cables

A third category is the heavy duty bolt and cable seals which are very strong and resist simple attack. They may be necessary where environmental security controls are poor but are disadvantaged by their relatively high cost and, sometimes, easy replication.

Cable types can be simply tampered if incorrectly fitted.

Electronic Seals

Finally it is only right to mention the new generation of electronic seals which are self-powered and are fitted as a permanent component of the load compartment or container. These are very effective when used on vehicle body doors and have been successfully used by in-house retail goods distributors. However, for the foreseeable future their high cost makes it unlikely that they will gain popularity in the large scale through transport arena where system standardisation and universally understood sealing methods are required.

Seal Audit and Checking

Once having chosen the right seal, it will not perform adequately unless subjected to a comprehensive system of practical check and administrative audit. To fit a seal at one juncture and to remove it at the next without any check or inspection, is to merely make a cosmetic gesture which has no security value whatsoever. Seal audit starts at manufacture where a multi-differ serial number must be applied. It is also common to find further identifiable marks applied to the batch such as the logo of the carrier but care should be taken not to apply marks which identify the type of cargo protected by the seal (a warning for users of "shippers own" seals). Care should be taken to arrange for secure delivery of bulk supplies of seals and to check that they are complete in sequence on receipt. Thereafter, any holding of bulk supplies must be held in physically secure conditions in order to deny access to unauthorised persons, particularly haulage drivers and container depot/terminal workers. The loss of seals from bulk supplies compromises the audit system and begs the need to issue invalid seal lists to all interchange points — these are difficult to administer and endanger the commercial reputation of the carrier.

The issue of seals in sequencially numbered batches to points of ready use must be carefully recorded. Individual seals must then be allocated to specific jobs and this recorded in a seal issue register. The better through transport operators provide a seal with each container despatched to the shipper. An exemplar seal issue register may be completed as follows:

Seal Number	Date	Container Number	Reason
492400	8 June 90	ABCU 0462347	FCL Export
492401	8 June 90	XYZU 0692497	FCL Export
492402	8 June 90	LMNU 0222349	Broken seal at gate
492403	8 June 90	XYZU 0929476	Import Customs Examination
492404	9 June 90	ABCU 0514972	FCL Export
492405	9 June 90	OPUU 0279888	FCL Re-seal after fumigation
492406	9 June 90	ABCU 0727463	LCL onward transit

This shows how the components of a seal audit trail are formed. The audit is then continued throughout the transit by interchange checks. These checks on the condition of the seal should be carried out by the agent receiving the sealed container as his record that the previous custodian has maintained integrity of the cargo. This is discussed further in Chapter 7.

The seal check comprises a visual inspection of the seal taking note of any obvious signs of abnormality; this may be cutting marks, signs of adhesive or distortion of the seal components. It is best also to handle the seal, to tug it in case it has been cut and replaced losely, or, in the case of a bolt seal, to rotate the shaft inside the barrel to ensure no repair has been carried out in order to reinstate the sealed condition.

Once satisfied that the seal is in good condition, it is essential that the serial number is recorded and retained. It may not be possible at all interchanges to verify that the seal number is the original as manifested but this is not so important as the contribution that is being made to the audit record which can be evaluated should an investigation ensue (see chapter 7). Typical interchange points at which seal checks should be carried out are as follows:—

Diag. 2 **TYPES OF LOAD COMPARTMENT**

2 x 20ft container mounted on 40ft skeletal or flat bed trailer. Solid steel boxes with barn type sealable doors at one end. Containers can also be mounted on a railway wagon or stacked on a ship or on the ground. Good physical security for high value loads.

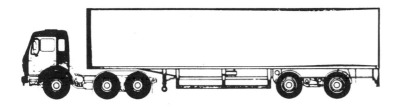

Box van. Solid construction, integral with the articulated trailer with various types of sealable doors at one end. Good physical security for high value loads.

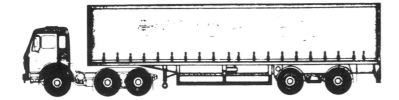

Curtain sided trailer. Solid construction with sealable doors at one end but soft skinned (fabric) sides with tension fasteners which can be sealed with a cord. Poor security for high value loads but if loading flexibility overrides, very high transit security environments and extended comprehensive interchange integrity checks required.

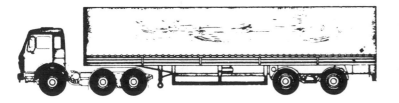

Tilt or Tautliner. Virtually flat bed trailer with completely soft skinned sides, ends and roof secured by a cord laced around the complete tilt and sealed at the rear. Poor security, as for curtain sided trailer (above).

(a)   Entrance gate of container depot or terminal (port or rail freight)

(b)   On collection from any point by a road haulier.

(c)   During stock checks of loaded containers in long term storage

(d)   On handover (receipt) from the rail freight system.

(e)   On board ship, during voyage (see chapter 4)

(f)   On discharge from a ship.

(g)   On delivery to final consignee (who should retain the removed seal in case of cargo complaint).

Thus it should be possible to trace the history of a seal from manufacture to final disposal. Also it is the means by which the integrity of the cargo is maintained and point of loss or damage traced in the event of a complaint or claim.

It is self evident that a degree of training is necessary for all staff who are required to use and check security seals.

Security of Goods Vehicles

When being transported by road, the security of cargo is synonymous with the security of the carrying vehicle. To a large extent, through transport security relies on the environmental controls which are exercised at the interchange points and the better carriers will avoid vehicles being parked and unattended when the cargo is on board. Whilst this can largely be avoided in practise there will be short periods, such as during drivers regulatory breaks away from his cab at, for example, motorway service stations. For fixed (box) bodied vehicles, vehicle electronic alarm systems can be extended to cover the load compartment but this is not the case for trailer loaded containers. Even so, there are very simple methods the driver can employ to prevent pilferage in his absence such as parking back to back with another vehicle or with the rear loading doors close up to a building, fence or wall. Soft skinned load compartments (known as tilts, tautliners, curtain siders) are vulnerable to simple attack by cutting a hole in the fabric. The transportation of high value or attractive cargo is not recommended utilising these vehicles unless there is an absolute guarantee that all interchange or parking places are high security areas. Even then, the interchange integrity check is complicated by the extension of the seal check to a check of the tilt cord and an inspection for damage or recent repair of the soft body.

It is still necessary to protect the complete vehicle from being driven away and whilst it will not be economical to always fit sophisticated electronic alarm systems, simple immobiliers such as air brake locks are effective and relatively inexpensive. If it is necessary to park a loaded articulated trailer for a short time, then the fitment of a fifth wheel lock (this prevents a tractor unit hitching up) is the most sensible precaution. Many of these methods will be considered necessary by hauliers to merely protect their equipment and carriers can take advantage by selecting hauliers who do take such care.

Haulage Contracts

It is sensible for through transport carriers to reinforce the standard terms and conditions of road haulage contractors by the issue of a specific contract document. This will detail the required standards of commercial practise, insurance, operational procedure, safety and security. It is the last of these with which we are concerned here and the following is a list of security requirements which should be included.

1.   **Vehicles**

(a)   Should have no broken locks, windows or other defects which would affect security

(b)   **High value Loads** — any security alarms or immobilisation devices should be fitted to British Standard 6803 part 3. Air brake locks should be fitted as a minimum requirement.

2. **Drivers**

   (a) Should have supplied references from previous employers (which the haulier has checked to source by telephone).

   (b) Should be issued with a company identity card incorporating a photograph and authorisation order.

3. **Driver Practise**

   (a) Never leave the vehicle unattended with keys in position or cab unlocked.

   (b) Keep both doors (driver and passenger) locked whilst in transit to prevent entry by thieves at temporary stops (e.g. at traffic lights).

   (c) Ensure container or load compartment is sealed and the seal number recorded. If no seal is fitted, make sure this is done by the shipper or previous agent in the chain before you depart.

   (d) Never leave keys hidden in vehicle or elsewhere for collection by relief.

   (e) Never park vehicle in secluded or unlit areas.

   (f) Do not pick up hitch hikers.

   (g) Do not reveal contents of load or parking intentions in discussions with third parties (e.g. in cafes).

   (h) Be wary of being followed either on foot, when returning to vehicle, or on the road.

   (i) If the vehicle breaks down, be wary of assistance from third parties.

   (j) If possible when parking, back up to obstacle to deny access to rear loading doors.

   (k) If stopped by "Police" stay in locked cab and indicate that you will follow them to the nearest police station.

   (l) When delivering a load
       (i) Do not agree to last minute changes of delivery address unless authorised by a self initiated telephone call to head office
       (ii) Do not terminate custody of the load or equipment (e.g. uncouple and leave a trailer) until in possession of authenticated P OD.

4. **Overnight Parking at Hauliers Premises**

   (a) The tractor unit must be disconnected from the trailer and locked/immobilised with the keys removed.

   (b) Tractor unit keys, kept at the yard, must be in a safe and securely locked place.

   (c) The yard must be enclosed by a continuous perimeter fence of adequate height and strength.

   (d) Gates must be manned by suitable security personnel or locked with a device that will withstand normal bolt croppers and with hinge pins securely capped or welded.

   (e) For high value loads, if the yard is unmanned the following are minimum requirements:
       (i) Environment monitored by video recorded CCTV system.
       (ii) Security contractor required to visit site randomly at least twice in each eight hour period.
       (iii) Trailer to be secured with fifth wheel lock and backed up to obstruction to prevent access to container doors.

Although major hauliers should be easily able to comply with such conditions, it is important to remember that sub-contracting is widespread and often necessary to accommodate last minute jobs in the interest of the carrier. This is when normal good security may be compromised and why it is important to hold the principal contractor tightly in contract to security standards which he must extend to his sub-contractors.

Monitoring Road Transits

For some high value loads it will be prudent to monitor road transits so as to be alerted early to any security incidents and to deter hi-jackers. There are various degrees of monitoring, starting with the despatching location simply being aware of how long a journey should take and alerting the receiving location of this so it can investigate if the vehicle is late. These days, many heavy goods vehicles are fitted with carphones and this allows for a driver to make check calls en route, say every hour for a journey taking more than two. The function of initiating check calls to these vehicles can be contracted out to a security central station where the staff will monitor the transits and, if any problem is signalled, alert the carrier or the police for appropriate action to be taken.

The ultimate in monitoring is for the vehicle to be escorted. This can range from two HGV's with similar loads/destinations travelling together on the road to the practise of covert escort by a security officer in a car. This can be the best method if loads of extremely high value need to the sent at regular times on regular routes. Sometimes this cannot be avoided if, for instance, the need is to co-ordinate with a specific ship sailing time each week and to prevent the cargo being stationary and vulnerable for a time at the port. Covert escorts are implemented so that the escort car does not appear to be associated with the HGV; this is so as not to present a dual target for hi-jackers. The HGV and escort can keep in touch by carphone and the drivers can take turns at having comfort breaks at service stations. This is not a particularly expensive operation but the need must be anticipated in order to allow for the cost in the freight rate. Most shippers of high value cargo will recognise the need, or even specify it, and regard the service as a valuable part of the carriers' overall service.

Illus · 4   Rail Freight Terminal

Chapter 4

Security of
Ships and their Cargo

SECURITY OF SHIPS AND THEIR CARGO

A friend once told me that ships do not need security because they have water around them. It is true that throughout the middle Ages, the moat was regarded as a standard and indispensable part of castle defences but this does not excuse the misconception by my friend; a ship and its' contents are vulnerable both at sea and also in port when they then become an extension of the land and raise many of the security problems common to large buildings.

There are a whole range of cargo ships used by the through transport industry. High value and attractive cargo however is usually shipped in either containers or vehicle/trailer load compartments and we will therefore concentrate on container ships, roll/on-roll/off vessels and ferries.

Ships in Port

The security required for a ship in port is very much related to the standard of shoreside security which exists. The latter is discussed in chapter five and is beginning to be regulated by the sort of legislation and international customs agreements mentioned in chapter one. Nevertheless, in many ports there is very little in the way of physical control and, for someone with a modicum of determination, it can then be perfectly possible to board an ocean going cargo ship and proceed to the most important parts of that ship unchallenged. This is why the stowaway problem is growing and why cargo pilferage and drug trafficking can be prepetrated covertly by intruders. It is also why, should terrorists begin to regard cargo ships as economic targets, we shall see a growth in the hijack and sabotage of these vessels unless there is more recognition of the need for an increase in the level of deterrents.

Illus·5   Container Ship

Let us consider the problem for the largest of container ships and firstly appreciate the sheer size of these vessels. This can be quantified in terms of "twenty foot equivalent units (teus)", which means their carrying capacity of containers which are twenty feet in length, although remember that containers are in both twenty and forty foot lengths. Typically, the modern generation of deep sea container tonnage can be over 3,500 teus, around 300 metres in length and the height of St. Paul's Cathedral in London. It is also the trend to operation these ships with the minimum of manpower and complements totalling twenty-five officers and crew are becoming normal. When in port there is not a great deal of employment for these personnel and for the usual turn around period of 24-48 hours or so they will be stood down and probably ashore for much of the time. In a home port, a crew change may be effected and on these occasions it is not uncommon for relatives and friends to visit and even stay overnight on board. Certainly, important areas such as the bridge may be vacant of staff for most of the period in port.

Gangway Security

The conventional method of pedestrian entrance to the ship is via the gangway. It is here where access to the ship must be controlled. There is a school of thought that this control can be effected by the crew but, although the officer of the watch must be involved, it is my firm belief that this function should be shore-based, i.e. provided by the ships' agent. The reasons are as follows:—

(a) The size of the ships complement does not allow sufficient capacity for dedication to the facility.

(b) The control must be continous and therefore it is best organised as a security guarding operation as described in chapter two.

(c) Control of crew access/egress (and that of their visitors) must be uncompromised.

(d) Access control records should be retained by the ships agent at the port.

(e) Where port security controls exist, there should be liaison based on local knowledge.

The objectives of gangway access control should be three fold. Namely:

(a) To provide a comprehensive retrospective record of who boarded or left the ship throughout it's stay in the port.

(b) At any particular time during the ship's stay, to provide an immediate identifiable headcount of those on board as a contingency measure in case of an emergency which may require a roll-call or an evacaution of all personnel. This headcount is also important immediately prior to sailing.

(c) To deter persons from boarding a ship for illegal purposes. (Remember that criminals invariably carry out reconnaissance and a properly guarded gangway may well convince them to go elsewhere).

The implementation of gangway access control should therefore be as follows:—

(a) Immediate implementation as soon as the ship berths and the gangway is lowered.

(b) Inclusive of all personnel however senior and no matter with what authority they board the ship.

(c) Comprehensive written register of those joining or leaving and recording the following details:

    (i)   Date
    (ii) Name
    (iii) Status, or Employer
    (iv) Reason for joining
    (v) Time of joining
    (vi) Time of leaving.

(d) Maintained continuously until the gangway is raised before sailing.

There are a number of practical considerations. Firstly, although there will be many individual visitors to a cargo ship, others will be in groups or form part of standard groupings. The crew themselves fall into this category and so do dock workers. The latter will often need to pass the gangway frequently and it is advisable to provide a more efficient way of recording or authorising these transits. The best method is to issue identity badges and insist that these are displayed. They must be dedicated to the wearer (e.g. name and photograph) but can be numbered in sets, particularly for crews. There is no claim however that these systems are easy to implement and administer.

The second consideration is that of communication and this is best achieved by hand held radio transceiver. The gangway guard must be able to contact the ships' office (duty officer) and also summon assistance from shore-side if required.

Thirdly, lighting is also an important consideration as it must be remembered that the function must carry on throughout the dark hours. The light source should come from the ship and either illuminate the area around the top of the gangway or be directed below to the level of the dock side. This question of positioning brings us to a very important problem. A container berth is by nature a dangerous place due to the cargo handling operation. It is therefore logical to position the gangway access control on board ship at the top of the walkway. Most ships lend themselves quite well to this arrangement when the entry to the ship is a covered way, thus providing some essential shelter and possibly a source of warmth for the guards. However, new tonnage, particularly that of economical far eastern design, often presents an open deck configuration at the top of the gangway. This means that there is not an adequate facility for access control other than at a further point into the ship. The problem is accentuated in bad weather and during winter nights. It also begs the question of how many personnel are required to mount a guard; frequent relief necessitated by harsh environmental conditions may force double manning, at double the cost. However, this is really a single man operation except at times of high volume movement such as during a crew change. There is no easy answer to the problem until access control to ships becomes a universally accepted standard at design stage and it is my belief that the situation will be another pressure point on terminal operators to provide secure berths for ships i.e. the access control, in the concentrated form necessary to protect vessels, will be applied shoreside.

Before leaving gangway security, we should make a passing mention of search. Given that anti-terrorism is not yet a primary aim for cargo shipping, the level of personnel search on gangways does not need to be routinely high. However, random inspection of items being hand carried, either on or off the ship, should be made to deter and detect both cargo pilferage and drug trafficking.

Cargo security at Sea

Again we will use the large container ship as the example for this subject. Bearing in mind the through transport chain, the ship represents a relatively long storage period for the containerised cargo. The risk of theft is that of pilferage and not of the complete container, although some surprisingly large proportions of FCL cargo have been misappropriated during voyages. In this context, remember that the ship will be carrying empty containers for return and re-supply purposes and the systematic unloading of FCL contents into an empty container (for subsequent plundering after discharge from the ship) can be possible during the voyage.

It will be clear from what has been said so far that crew are primary candidates for criminal suspicion when such pilferage takes place. Unfortunately, experience shows that this suspicion is entirely justified although these are of course other possible perpetrators. These include stowaways, whose majority is popularly believed to consist of adventurers but in fact is predominately made up of political refugees, delinquents avoiding custodial sentences and prostitutes. The effect of extremely large ships operated by extremely small crews is that the opportunity for a stowaway to remain undetected is high. Some stowaway activity is organised and there was recently a case whereby a lady travelled safely from Europe to South Africa in an "empty" container equipped with both rations and toilet facilities sufficient for the 3 week voyage. Other examples of unofficial seafarer's are the boat people of the Suez Canal who board ships for the up to 24 hour transit of the canal in order to market their merchandise to the ships' company.

The next thing to establish is that containerised cargo can be accessed and removed when stowed on board. Firstly, containers are stacked up to three high on deck and, whilst the second and third tiers are difficult to access, the doors of the boxes at deck level can be opened fully. Secondly, containers are stacked underdeck, up to nine deep and there are many positions where their doors can be opened to a variable degree. Container ship owners should survey their ships and produce annotated bay plans, such as the one illustrated here, to identify the vulnerable spaces. The reasons are twofold:

Diag. 3 EXAMPLE CONTAINER SHIP BAY PLANS SHOWING VARYING DEGREES OF ACCESS TO CONTAINER DOORS

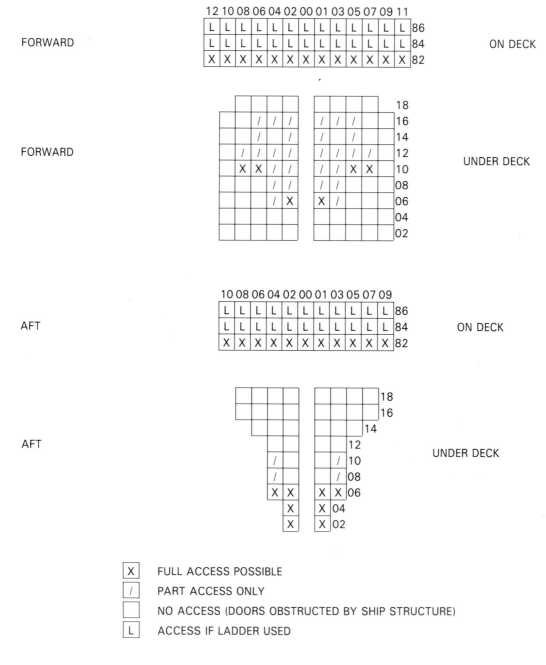

X	FULL ACCESS POSSIBLE
/	PART ACCESS ONLY
	NO ACCESS (DOORS OBSTRUCTED BY SHIP STRUCTURE)
L	ACCESS IF LADDER USED

(a) To evaluate which areas of the ship should be physically secured at sea.

(b) To demonstrate the balance of probability when cargo loss claims result in point of loss liability actions.

Obviously, the majority of shipboard pilferage is aimed at valuable and attractive cargo from which small quantities are worth removing. Examples are electronic products, wines and spirits, cigarettes, cosmetics and clothing. Unfortunately, it is not a practical proposition to allocate such cargoes to secure bay positions when formulating the load plan, indeed one of the protective principles of containers is that they are anonymous in the sense of value and that their external appearance anduniversal handling deny criminal targetting. This is not to say that special arrangements cannot be made for a small number of high risk containers such as those carrying bullion or weapons, but attractive cargo such as that previously mentioned, can form a large proportion of the loads shipped, say, between Europe and the Far East.

There is however a need to prevent unauthorised knowledge of container contents during a voyage. A primary method is to avoid carrying a fully detailed cargo manifest on board. There is no need for a ship to have these documents, other than to beware of the presence of hazardous cargo, because the details can be communicated for administrative purposes between the ports of call in good time before the ship arrives at each one. Should a full manifest be on board however, and they can be introduced gratuitously by agents at transhipment ports, it must be secured in the masters safe and not left lying in the ships' office for all to see.

The introduction of micro computers to ships also presents a confidentiality risk in the respect of cargo identity. It should be remembered, by those of us who have seen this equipment develop well after the years of our youth, that even an employee of quite low standing may these days have accomplished computer literacy at school. The ships' load plan file does not reveal cargo type but it will detail container weight, port of origin/destination and stow position. Sea staff on the look-out for attractive cargo may deduce this from the load plan data. For example, a forty foot FCL with relative low weight/capacity ratio and booked Tokyo to Southampton, may well contain electronic goods such as video cameras. If the bay position renders the container doors accessible then the opportunity for theft is good.

The answer to micro computers security on board is one of physical protection:

(a) Equipment should be fitted with hardware locks such as keyboard locks and power supply inhibitors, the keys for these should be secured or kept personally by the authorised user (e.g. First Officer).

(b) Software locks should be employed such as user identity and file access passwords.

(c) The computer should never be left running whilst unattended by its authorised user.

(d) Software should be locked away if removed from the computer.

Incidentally, these precautions will also prevent the unauthorised use of the computer, for example playing games, which could corrupt vital programmes.

There are also other indicators to cargo identity, such as a container bearing inflammable liquid warning stickers and loaded at Le Havre, may well be a cargo of brandy. Security seals are also an indicator although the industry is seeking to use a universal standard which will improve cargo anonymity as explained in Chapter three.

Nevertheless, if the thief has a choice between a container secured with a common strip seal and one bearing a heavy duty bolt, and perhaps additionally customs sealed, then the latter may prove more fruitful. Some cargo manufacturers insist on using their own seals which are inscribed with the company name or logo; this can be a giveaway. Much of the preventative action required is basic physical security. In concert with safety considerations, hold areas should be locked when no one is required to be there. It should be remembered that most of the ships' complement will just complete a normal working day, during a deep sea leg, and when they cease work in the evening, return to their accommodation or to the ship's leisure facilities. There may only be a couple of men on duty on the bridge during the 'silent hours'. At this time, work in the holds would be unusual and the presence of personnel under deck would beg investigation. A combination of physically locking hold access points and the provision of electronic alarms to, say, the water tight doors in the side passages, which activate audible warnings to the bridge are positive means of deterrence and crime prevention. Suited locks should be fitted and the master key held only by one officer who should be in exclusive charge of key control.

The problem on deck is not so simple and although there have been feasability studies of various methods by which the doors on containers stowed in deck level spaces could be mechanically obstructed none of these have so far been successful. The answer here is to apply routine monitoring of the cargo by senior officers inspection. It is part of the masters responsibility to ensure that his cargo is safe and secure and so a physical patrol of the deck, systematically transversing each walkway between the stacked containers, should be carried out soon after each sailing. The security element of this inspection is to check that container doors are closed and that the seals are intact. From a carriers' liability viewpoint this is an important interchange check on the integrity of sealed containers received from the terminal. Obviously, the only seals that can be thoroughly checked will be those at deck level but a visual inspection of seals on higher tiers will be possible and have some meaning if the shipper uses seals which accord with the guidance given in chapter three.

This type of inspection should also be extended to the underdeck cargo where it can be accessed, albeit a lengthly job. Here again, seals which are brightly coloured and would not stay affixed if tampered come into their own. Any seals which are found to be missing or broken on loaded containers must be replaced. The ship therefore needs a ready use supply of carriers' seals and an issue register where re-sealing can be properly recorded to form part of the seal audit trail.

Although these inspections have been described as interchange checks, it is also good policy to repeat them perhaps covering partial sectors, on a random basis throughout the voyage. This is the way in which cargo interference by sea staff, or by dock workers in particular ports of call, is discovered and, through methodology, deterred.

A sharp eye should also be kept to identify small quantities of cargo which may have been "hidden" by thieves until the time at which they intend to remove them from the ship. Theft from containers underdeck is often a hazardous pursuit and the perpetrators do accidentally drop items; take care to observe the areas of the hull immediately below the container bays for evidence of this.

The question of removal of pilfered cargo from the ship raises the issue of how this can be done. Although we have dealt with gangway security in some detail, there are other methods of entering and leaving the ship. It is not my intention to dwell on this because the primary aim here is to "close the stable door before the horse bolts." However, some examples for enlightenment are as follows:

(a) Riding off in empty containers

(b) Via small boat or other vessel from the seaward side in port

(c) Via the rubbish skip put aboard at most ports

(d) Via the stores crane which is also often used to discharge personal baggage during crew changes.

Also, it should not be assumed that crew who have pilfered cargo will remove this at a home port or during a crew change. In ports where terminal security is poor it has been known for sea staff to mail large parcels home from, say, the seaman's mission. Of course, collusion with dock workers is not uncommon and these variables do beg the need for preventative security in the first place.

Cargo Security on Ferries and Roll on-Roll off Vessels

Through transport operations involving ferries utilise a variety of carrying modes, from containers and their fixed (box body) equivalents to vehicles and trailers with soft-skinned load compartments known variously as tilts, taut liners and curtain siders. Because the means of coneyance is travelling (unlike on a container ship), there are two kinds of transit, namely, accompanied and unaccompanied. The former is where the driver is common door to door and travels as a foot passenger on the same ferry.

The latter is where one driver delivers the trailer to the export port, it is then drawn aboard the ship by the ferry operator and collected at the import port by another driver who hauls it onward. The vulnerability of the load to interference during the voyage varies according to the time scale of the crossing. For example, Dover to Calais is potentially safer than Portsmouth to St. Malo. The standard ruling is that no passenger is permitted to stay on the vehicle decks during the voyage and this should be enforced rigorously by the crew. Soft skinned load compartments are of course easy to slash and this allows for swift pilferage. The other weakness is that unless the sealing cord is laced through each eyelet and drawn tight to the sealing point, there is always the chance of illicit access to the load from beneath the curtain.

Some considerable security advantage to the shipper is gained by accompanied operations because the driver, whose door to door responsibility is self evident, will check his vehicle and load for obvious interference whenever he returns to it after a short period of absence (such as at the end of a ferry crossing). Unaccompanied loads are consequently due less attention making interchange checking at either endof the ferry operation (including any periods spent in port trailer parks) essential from the liability viewpoint.

It follows from this appraisal that the identification of load interference during the transit of soft bodied vehicles is less precise than when containers are involved and when the condition of the seal is the main indicator. The lesson for shippers of high value, attractive and highly pilferable cargo is that soft skinned load compartments are much less secure and really quite unsuitable for unaccompanied ferry operations. There sometimes has to be a compromise where back loading/unloading facilities and loading bays are not available at either end of the transit. It is then that the implementation of comprehensive interchange security checks are paramount and should be regarded as an advantage to all concerned.

Anti-drug trafficking Sea carrier Agreement Procedures

These procedures include effective access control to ships when in port as covered earlier in this chapter. Following on, they then involve a very positive effort related to the responsibility of the master whilst at sea. As far as the carrier is concerned, he should ensure compliance with the customs agreement by a formal delegation to the master in the form of written procedures.

Clearly where ships are very large, fully comprehensive cover is impossible, particularly if crew are involved as drug users or couriers. Preventative action on board is therefore addressed by random action but this can be directed to geographical areas or in places on the ship where the risk is greatest. The geographical aspect is not easy these days because although source countries for drugs (e.g. South America) are fairly well known, the ingenuity of organised traffickers causes them to confuse the issue by devious distribution routes through areas of the world generally thought to be of low risk. Transhipment ports all over the world are therefore vulnerable loading points. From a commercial viewpoint, and in terms of reducing the risk of customs penalties, masters must be encouraged to increase their awareness of the problem when the next call is to agreement countries such as the USA and New Zealand.

In port, masters should be alert to swimmers or small boats close to the ship. When ships' provisions and spares are being boarded, this should be a supervised operation. Items such as bottled gas, water canisters and fire extinguishers (which lend themselves to drug smuggling) should be examined. Areas of the ship such as spare cabins which are not frequented regularly should be locked or sealed to deter surreptitious concealment of drug consignments.

Where crew may be involved, the master must be alert to behavioural patterns which may be consistent with trafficking. For example:

(a) Unusually large amounts of money

(b) Unusually high level of legal purchasing.

(c) Expensive clothing

(d) Association with persons ashore in ports where the crew member seldom visits

(e) Unusual dress when going ashore such as out of season or bulky clothing

(f) Unnatural interest in a particular part of the ship

(g) Unnatural interest in a particular container.

Worse, where crew may be drug users as well (also a risk to the safe running of the ship), the following may be tell-tale signs:

(a) Nervousness

(b) Anti-social or irrational behaviour

(c) Frequent unexplained movements

(d) Radical changes in work habits or lifestyle

(e) Slurred speech, sweating, glazed eyes.

However, the most important procedures are those involving surveillance and search. They are also activities which can be recorded in the ships' log and this is an essential element in the formulation of a case mitigation following penalty imposition. Surveillance can be carried out during routine ship inspections and can include a lookout for drug users paraphernalia in crew cabins, the existence of unusual odours, evidence of a remote area of the ship being frequented or interference with a container seal. Searches are more formal and can range from the master and first officer concentrating on a small area to an organised team search of a section such as the Deck Department, Stewards Department or Engineering Department. These will involve a planned approach and include the close inspection of places such as:

(a) Ventilation ducts

(b) Equipment boxes

(c) Lifeboat storage areas

(d) Behind toilets

(e) Under catwalks.

The above is not intended to be an exhaustive list and a properly prepared formal instruction on the subject should include a search plan with annexed lists of places which, if systematically examined, will represent a comprehensive search. Crew who are involved in drug trafficking will be significantly deterred from doing so in ships where such procedures are normal.

There are however three aspects of search by ships officers which I reserve the right to be extremely cautious in recommending, despite their requirement by the United States Customs. These are:

(a) The personal search of a crew member.

(b) The detailed search of a cabin in the absence of its occupant

(c) The extent of area search which involves dismantling of components or structure.

The first two are difficult because of the legal rights of the individual and because of the legal requirements of procedure if subsequent prosecution is to be successful and if subsequent legal action of complaint against the searcher are to be avoided. It is enough to summarise by saying that these measures are best left by commercial companies to trained security officers whose expertise is unlikely to be part of the experience of a ships officer.

The third aspect, that of the extent of search, is largely one of the capacity of a busy ships complement to devote the necessary time to such activity. It may be one thing to briefly lift a polystyrene tile to view a false ceiling void but entirely another to dismantle a complete length of trunking in the side passage. There is also an insidious risk here because it is a well known practise of those who conceal packages of drugs, to include a booby trap device such as a sharp instrument in the access point to the hiding place. This is designed to cause such injury to the searcher which dissuades him from further exploration which may reveal the hidden item. It is perhaps unsafe to invite such a fate to personnel who are not employed primarily to engage in the discovery of crime.

Customs officers and policemen are paid to take risks and it may be regarded as valid defence in mitigation of the drug trafficking penalty if a carrier has decided to limit the extent to which its employees are involved in counter measures, on the ground of safety.

Finally, should a quantity of suspected drugs be discovered on board the ship, handling of it should be avoided, the area of the find quarantined (if possible) and the find notified ahead to the customs authority at the next port of call.

Chapter 5

Security of Cargo Interchange Establishments

SECURITY OF CARGO INTERCHANGE ESTABLISHMENTS

The integrity of the through transport chain relies heavily on the physical security arrangements at cargo interchange establishments. Examples of these locations are as follows:

(a) Cargo storage and handling areas at Seaports

(b) Freight consolidation and distribution centres

(c) Inland Clearance Depots (ICD's)

(d) Trailer and Lorry Parks

(e) Railway Freight Terminals

(f) Warehouses

(g) Haulage Yards

Whilst we will highlight the special problems associated with these various types of location, the main aim of this chapter will be to detail the basic security measures required and to show how best they may be achieved. In this way we will satisfy commercial needs and, at the same time embrace the requirements of maritime security legislation and of customs regulations for bonded cargo and inland clearance. Reference should therefore be made to the diagram of a typical cargo transit depot. This represents a totally enclosed high security area with continuous guarding and control of access and egress. There are two main security risks to the cargo at this location, namely:—

(a) Pilferage, principally by intruders

(b) Theft of a full load by deception.

Diag. 4   **TYPICAL CARGO TRANSIT DEPOT SECURITY**

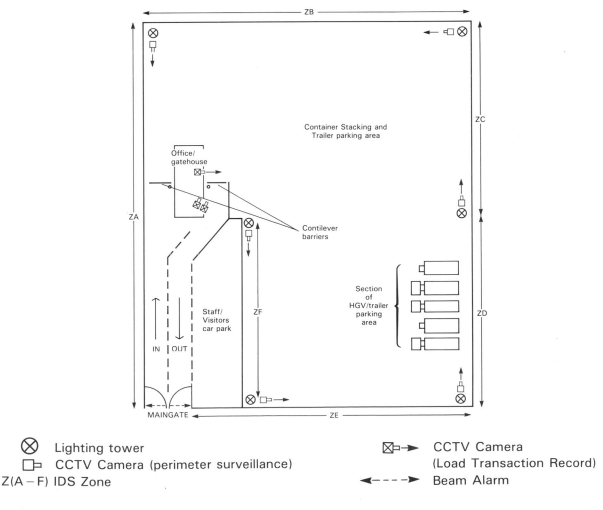

⊗ Lighting tower

▢⊐ CCTV Camera (perimeter surveillance)

Z(A – F) IDS Zone

⊠⊐→ CCTV Camera (Load Transaction Record)

◄- - -► Beam Alarm

Intrusion by thieves should be dealt with by a combination of perimeter defences with surveillance systems monitored by security guards and continuous documentary procedures, control of egress from the site and video recording. The integrity of the sealed containers or load compartments on site is maintained by interchange checks at the entrance gate and on collection. This represents a total contribution to the security audit trail.

Perimeter Defences

The delination of the site boundary is usually achieved by fencing. The security objectives are:

(a)   To deter and delay intrusion

(b)   To facilitate installation of IDS (Intruder Detection System).

It follows that the fence must be of sufficient height, sufficient rigidity and (a major commercial consideration) resistant to accidental damage and natural deterioration. Security fences should be at least 3 metres high. They can be topped with barbed wire, spread or coiled between extension posts which are best in the vertical plane and not, as is commonly seen, cranked either inwards or outwards. Conventional chain link panels should be avoided due to their tendancy to collapse when the tensioners or links are cut and because of their poor performance after impact. Welded mesh fences are much stronger and have greater longevity, but the state of the art now offers best all round performance from steel palisade fencing. This type also has steel posts which provide better resistance to impact damage (common in areas of container handling and heavy vehicle movement) than the conventional concrete variety which break easily. Gate construction should be of equivalent standard to the fence. The hinges should be able to resist removal of the complete gate and the bottom of the gate should not clear the ground by more than 50mm.

The fence also provides the means of mounting the IDS (intruder detection system). There are various types of perimeter IDS but most are of limited effectiveness because of environmental variations. The most important requirements to remember are that:

(a)   They should have low false alarm rates

(b)   Alarm activations should be easy to evaluate

(c)   They should not be activated by normal site operations.

Given these three considerations, experience shows that fence mounted acoustic wire types are most useful. This is because they produce an audible signal which can, with experience, indicate to the guard (who monitors the control equipment) what type of event has activated the system. For example, it is relatively easy to tell the difference between natural events, like high winds or rodent movement, and the more suspicious such as cutting or climbing disturbance. It can be seen from the diagram that the system is zoned so as to indicate the location of the activiation and, in my recommended solution, CCTV (closed circuit television) is used to provide a visual evaluation of the cause. Correct monitoring of these systems produces a very low incidence of false alarm and avoids the attendant waste of an unnecessary response.

The main gates of such sites will remain open for a large proportion of the time. They may only be locked closed for a few hours in the middle of the night and perhaps for a longer period during part of the weekend. When they are secured by the security guard, this should be achieved by a high quality padlock of the closed shackle variety which denies cutting by bolt croppers. As a guide, the 1990 price of such locks is around £70; anything costing relatively less than this figure is probably inadequate.

When the gates are open to allow vehicle movement, a simple alarm system should be installed which activates if there is movement through the gate. This is usually achieved by the transmission of an electronic beam which, when interrupted, signals an audible warning to the guard in the gatehouse. The main advantage of this is to warn the guard of any approaching traffic during times of low volume operation. Vehicle access in and out of the secure area is controlled by cantilever barriers which should remain in the lowered position at all times other than when a vehicle has been authorised to pass. This is a major point of discipline at such sites and should not be relaxed. It is worth mentioning that such barriers are extremely reliable in the technical sense but can be easily damaged by careless drivers. There are more robust barriers such as road blockers, which raise and lower from below ground level. However, these are very expensive to install and, in winter snow conditions, can become troublesome due to obstruction of the recess. On balance, the cantilever barriers are most cost effective.

Lighting

Artificial illumination of these sites is necessary for operational and safety reasons during the hours of darkness. The security value of this illumination can be realised during silent periods when the main objectives are:

(a) To deter intruders

(b) To observe intruders

(c) To provide support for CCTV systems.

The third of above reasons has cost advantages which too often go unrecognised. CCTV cameras are frequently assisted by infra-red illuminators which boost performance in the dark. The effect of these illuminators is impressive but their power consumption is considerable and the life of infra-red bulbs relatively short. Infra-red bulbs are expensive to replace both in terms of material and labour costs (a service call), so these illuminators should be avoided unless:

(a) Conventional illumination would cause a public nuisance

(b) A public roadway is adjacent to the site (when traffic safety would be compromised by bright lights)

(c) Covert surveillance is required.

It is far better to support CCTV systems with sufficient conventional lamps which also provide illumination for safe site operations.

The best type of lighting equipment is difficult to advise on in general terms because of the environmental variations of each location. Specialist local advice is therefore necessary but there is one simple practical point to remember. I have, on a number of occasions, surveyed sites where the illumination has been inadequate and supplementary equipment is under consideration. Before such consideration is made, always ensure that the lenses of existing lamps are cleaned; my experience is that this is often all that is required to restore adequate performance.

Closed Circuit Television

CCTV systems are perhaps the most effective aids to good security on through transport sites. Combined with continuous video recording they offer maximum deterrent to criminal acts by both intruders and staff and can easily be "sold" to the latter (even in trade unionised situations) on the basis of providing an accurate record of events and thus preventing unfounded suspicion after security incidents have occured. From the operational management viewpoint these systems also provide routine audit of normal business activity outside the pure security consideration.

At our typical site, CCTV has been utilised in two separate functions.

(a) Security of the perimeter and the rear doors of trailer mounted load compartments, **(surveillance)**

(b) Load transaction record at the exit gate **(event recording)**

Surveillance is the monitoring of an area for unusual activity and for the evaluation of alarm activations. The diagram shows the positioning of a series of fixed cameras each of which observes a length of site perimeter leading to the next camera in line. The IDS zones correspond to these and allow the system operator to select visual examination of the area appropriate to alarm activation. Additional cameras could also be used to view internal areas of the site if required.

It is worth emphasising that fixed cameras (those which only provide a pre-determined view) have been deliberately specified. This is because fully functional (PTZ) cameras (those which can be panned, tilted and zoom in on the subject by remote control) are three times as expensive and are open to abuse by operators. This is not to say that sometimes these PTZ types can be applied to great effect and economy, but in general terms, and particularly when event recording is important, it is better for the specifier to have total control over the picture that is viewed. This is also vital when sites are near to private property where occupants' complaints about "spying" can result in enforced deactivation of the system. We will discuss the selection of equipment in a later section but one technical tip is to recognise that camera technology has developed very rapidly over recent years. Only recently has solid state electronics replaced the tubed cameras to produce the charged coupled device (CCD) type. These have great reliability, longevity and consistant performance throughout their life. Apart from very specialist surveillance requirements (unlikely to be needed by readers of this book) it is my firm recommendation that CCD cameras should always be specified; beware suppliers with old stocks of tubed cameras at knocked-down prices.

Event recording, in the context of our typical site, is used to record the transactions of loads leaving the site. Two cameras view the front of the vehicle as it waits for release at the exit barrier. One of these records the description of the tractor unit or cab (including the registration index number) and the other records the description of the load compartment (e.g. the container or trailer box van number). A third camera, the most useful in terms of crime prevention or detection, is mounted in the wall of the gate house and provides a close-up picture of the drivers' features as he negotiates with the gate house staff. All three cameras simultaneously record on video tape to produce audit proof of load interchange and admissable legal evidence in the event of a vehicle or complete load theft.

Specification of Security Equipment

The security equipment market is in fantastic growth. A problem for the consumer is that the smart salesman with "technical security consultant" printed on his visiting card could easily have been merchandising confectionery last month. Security systems should therefore be specified and quantified before suppliers and installers are invited to provide proposals and quotations. It is the job of the directly employed security manager or genuinely qualified independent consultant to plan and state the operational requirements and general specification of the equipment. It is therefore a mistake to assume the security expertise of an equipment contractor. He should be regarded only as a technical adviser on how to achieve the security plan. Failure to realise this invariably leads to over specification and excessive costs. Account should also be taken of the need to specify standard products, even by manufacturer, so that a known reliability factor can be built in and availability of spare parts be secured in the long term. Care should also be taken to avoid hybrid system infrastructure.

The selection of Contractors

The selection of potential contractors should take account of the following:

(a) Known ability to install to the required standard (preferably British Standard)

(b) Geographically disposed in a manner which will ensure satisfactory after sales service, such as:

(i) Rectification response within 6 hours, 24 hours per day 365 days per annum

(ii) Minumum usage of sub-contractors

(iii) Use of standardised system test methods.

The Tender Board

At least three contractors should be asked to quote and it is best to brief them at a collective, formally arranged, briefing session. This will save time and should ensure standardised proposals which can be properly compared. Before placing an order with the successful contractor, he should be asked to demonstrate system components on site and provide a video tape of the results which can be held against the quality expected at commissioning and to be satisfied before settlement of the final invoice. It is surprising how often this method results in the identification of incorrect equipment specification or positioning and enables these to be rectified before final installation.

Security Procedures

At our typical site we will assume that all security procedures are to be allocated to security staff, but there are some of these where transport operations staff could be equally well employed. There are however two points of guidance here:

    (a)   Security staff expect to work unsocial hours and, if contracted, are relatively cheap labour

    (b)   In terms of contractual liability, it is best to allocate security duties to staff from the same source, so that the discontinuity which can result from hand over between directly employed and contract staff does not lead to dispute when attributing the responsibility for a security lapse.

            We should also recall the advice given in chapter 2 about the number of contracted security hours which should be purchased; far better value and quality of service will be obtained if 24 hour cover (i.e. 168 hours per week) is provided because full time, dedicated personnel can be supplied.

Security procedures at our typical site fall into two categories:

    (a)   Physical security of the site

    (b)   Reception and receipt of loads.

Physical security at the perimeter is addressed variably according to the time of day and is related to the operational pattern of the site. For example, if the site is a trailer park near to a seaport terminal, the the arrival of export loads and the shunting of these to and from the docks may go on for up to 18 of the 24 weekday hours. When the site is working and employees are in the operational areas, there is less need to patrol or observe perimeters and worry about intruders. This is not to say that continuous video recording is unnecessary; this is a deterrent to anyone, including staff, considering an illegal act. However, the security staff will have more physical security work to carry out in the truely silent hours, when the main gate can be closed and locked. It is the extent to which security systems (CCTV, IDS. etc) have been deployed which now determines the number of security staff required and whether or not they need to foot patrol as opposed to just monitor the systems. Even so, I am a great believer in full utilisation of staff and here is an example where security guards can be effectively used in a combined role.

The normal way of ensuring and recording foot patrols is by the use of clocking points where, either by mechanical or electronic means, the patrol is logged at points around the site and proof of completion provided in some form of print-out. At our typical site, there is a most effective way to do this by requiring the guard to carry out a physical stock check of stored/parked loads during the silent hours. He may be required to make a written record of all vehicle/trailer/container numbers and also to check seal integrity and numbers. If HGV refuelling facilities are provided on site, then meter readings can be taken. If refrigerated cargo is on site then checks can be made on consistant running of the freezer units. This procedure not only forces a very thorough patrol presence but also provides the site manager with a useful audit of assets. Should it be decided that foot patrols are unnecessary or unsafe, then the night guard should be required to "patrol" the site by systematically monitoring the pictures from each CCTV camera at regular intervals and recording these "patrols" in a written log. Contracted guards will also be required to make and receive telephone check calls to their employer's central station and to log any incident or visit to the site. They may also have custody of door, gate and vehicle keys and be required to issue these to authorised persons.

Reception and release of loads must be the subject of disciplined procedures. There must be no exception to these for every transaction. On arrival of a load, reception documentation will need to be completed but the most important aspect is the physical integrity check of the loaded vehicle. This is the first step of each link in the seal audit trail for it is the receiver of the load whose responsibility it is at each interchange point. With containers or box vans, given that there is no obvious damage or rupture of the load compartment (including the roof), it is the rear door locking mechanism and seal which is the focus of attention. The check of the seal must be as described in chapter 3 and a written record made of its' serial number. It is not essential for this number to be checked against the record of manifested seal number because any discrepancy would be discovered on subsequent investigation of the complete audit trail.

Should the seal or any other aspect be found insecure, then this fact should be recorded by the security guard who would also record the fitment of a new seal and inform the delivery driver.

With soft skinned load compartments (tilts, taut liners and curtain-siders) there are additional points to check:

(i)   Inspect the fabric for damage or obviously recent patch repair.

(ii)   Inspect the entire length of the sealing cord for fracture or jointed repair.

(iii) Ensure that the sealing cord is correctly laced through each eyelet of the fabric and also check for knotting techniques which would allow slackening of the cord without disturbance of the seal.

Load release is the security discipline applied to vehicles leaving the site. At our typical site the driver will have stopped at the lowered exit gate barrier and in line with the "drivers features" video camera. This time the security guard does not need to physically inspect the load other than to check that the load description (container/trailer number) matches the details on his pre-warned release documentation (this will also be auditable on video tape). He does need additionally to check that the haulage company, vehicle index number and driver's details match the documentation. As far as seal and load compartment integrity are concerned, on this occasion it is the driver's responsibility, as the receiving agent, to check these and report any irregularities before departure. There is a procedural variation when the driver is merely collecting empty equipment (container or trailer) together with documentation which authorises him to collect a load from a shipper and then carry it to another location. In this case all the previously mentioned checks apply except for the seal which this time is issued to the driver with his collection notes.

The guard must check that the serial number of the seal is the same as written on the documentation. The driver will give the seal to the shipper or consignor who should fit it to the load compartment when full. The driver should never be allowed to carry out this fitment but should sign the shippers receipt to the effect that he has collected a sealed load, with the correct seal number.

It is worth mentioning here that sometimes a shipper will wish to fit his own seal of a type which fills the majority of the sealing aperature and physically precludes the fitment of the carriers' seal. The driver's further responsibility now is to clause the documents to the effect that the carriers' seal was not fitted and to ensure safe return of the unused seal to the point of issue. It is good security practise, under site search agreements, to periodically search HGV cabs for unused seals which could otherwise be used to compromise the seal audit trail and aid surreptitious pilferage. All the procedures mentioned should be the subject of written standard operating instructions for the site. If security guarding is contracted in, the procedures should be reflected in the Assignment Instructions which form a contractual annex to the Service Agreement. This will be vital in the event of a liability case arising out of the loss of cargo or equipment.

Diag. 5   **TYPICAL SEAPORT CARGO TERMINAL**
(WITHIN DOCK AREA)

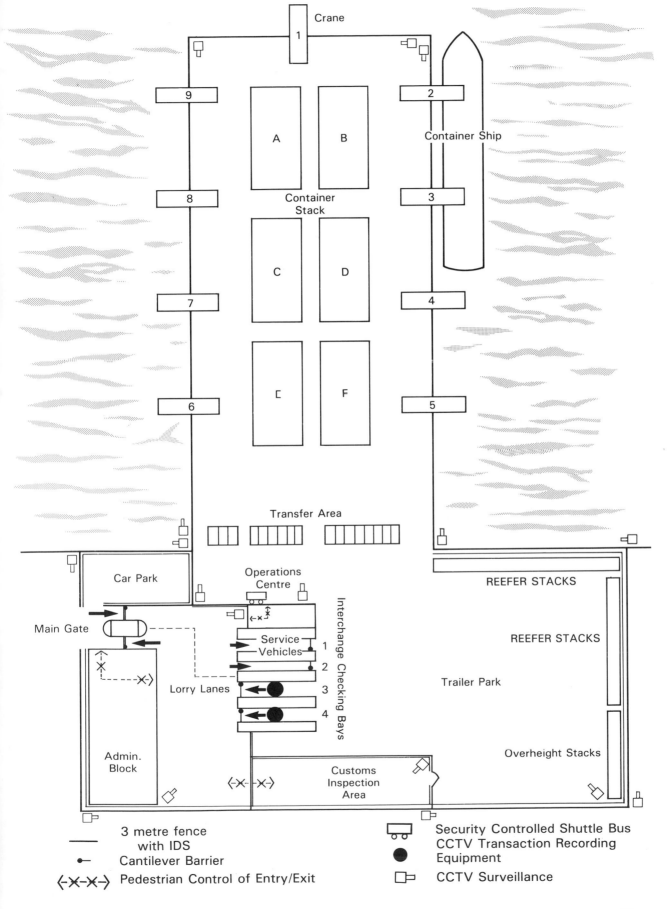

From time to time, the load compartments of empty vehicles leaving the site should be searched for unauthorised contents.

Leaving our typical site aside now, but regarding its security facility as the quality standard, we should consider the additional requirements peculiar to some of the establishment types listed at the beginning of this chapter.

Seaports

Given that there are commercial security needs for port areas, the new UK anti-terrorist legislation, mentioned in chapter one, introduces a further dimension. It enables the Department of Transport to issue certain directives to harbour authorities, to persons conducting business in harbour areas, to persons allowed into the restricted zone of a harbour area to conduct their business and to owners, managers, charterers or masters of ships. Under these directives, the Secretary of State can require:

(a) The designation of Restricted Zones within Port Areas.

(b) Searches of harbour areas, ships and persons and property within them, and of land and property outside harbour areas which is used for the purposes of businesses within them.

(c) The prevention of people and property from boarding ships and ships from sailing, unless searches have been carried out.

(d) The institution of any other general measures considered necessary, including the provision of guards, to protect ships and harbour areas from acts of violence.

(e) The appointment of Authorised Persons, with power of entry to inspect and test property, require information, and detain ships.

It is quite clear that this law covers not only the activities of those directly connected with ships and ports but also those of shippers, forwarding agents and road and rail transport companies. It is likely that approved lists will be produced of companies whose security procedures are adequate and this may be particularly relevant through future legislation covering freight transiting the Channel Tunnel. If anyone has any doubt about the terrorist threat to cargo operations, consider the effect of an explosive device discharging inside a maritime container at sea or even a relatively small explosion near to hazardous freight on land.

In addition to the need for secure premises and disciplined procedures, there will be a requirement for port operators to introduce identity pass systems for all employees and business visitors. This will involve the security administration necessary to issue, control and check these passes and will bring into play the employment of security staff as described elsewhere in this book.

One thing is certain, it will not be possible to wait for specific government directives based on heightened security threat assessment although these can be the signal to enforce security control with increased vigour. The basic element of physical and procedural security as broadly recommended in these pages will need to become the normal. It is not possible to build fences and install systems overnight and civilian security guarding companies do not have large forces of reserve manpower waiting to be mobilised with just a few hours, or days, notice.

Freight Consolidation Centres and Warehouses

The collection of small quantities of freight for loading together in containers or large vehicle load compartments and the reverse of this process for distribution purposes, necessitates the use of covered warehouses within secure cargo areas. This involves loose cargo handling and the need for very strict inventory controls during the process. It is also a time when freight packaging is vulnerbale to damage giving rise to opportunist theft of small attractive items by staff. The conventional way of deterring this is for security staff to patrol the working areas and observe all activities. They can also be used to provide authoritative tally of cargo on loading and unloading. However, the utilisation of security systems is much more economical and they are of course less corruptible than human beings. Large areas can be effectively covered by ceiling mounted fully functional CCTV cameras linked to control room monitors and continuously video recorded. Retail (shop) security techniques can be adapted for this purpose such as the concealment of a camera unit in a globe so that the direction of view cannot be seen from below. In warehouses with aisles between stacked columns of cargo, there is equipment which can be wall mounted and consists of a CCTV camera riding on a track and concealed by one way mirror glass. The single camera can travel the full length of the warehouse and watch working operations between each row of cargo in turn.

These types of establishments do require staff search clauses to be inserted into contracts of employment and for random searches to be carried out from time to time. Such personal searches of employees and their private vehicles must be conducted by trained security staff because of the code of practice demanded by the law. Suffice to say that search in these circumstances can only commence or continue with the current consent of the subject and the judgement required from the searchers can be only derived safely from previous formal law enforcement experience.

Diag. 6   **TYPICAL WAREHOUSE**

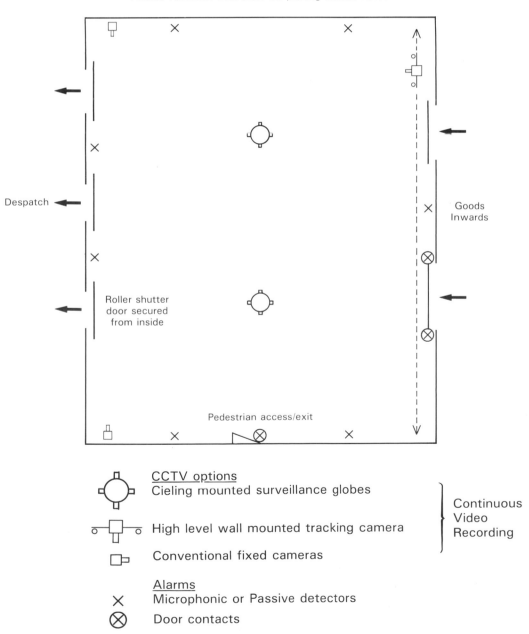

Fenced Perimeter with staff car parking outside fence

Despatch

Goods Inwards

Roller shutter door secured from inside

Pedestrian access/exit

CCTV options
Cieling mounted surveillance globes

High level wall mounted tracking camera

Conventional fixed cameras

Continuous Video Recording

Alarms
X   Microphonic or Passive detectors
⊗   Door contacts

Warehouses also need physical protection during the silent hours and, once empty of employees and secured, should be alarmed. The types of suitable alarm are many and various and to give specific advice here is difficult due to the different building configuerations which may be encountered. However, although passive detectors (which sense movement) are extremely popular, the use of microphonic systems which transmit sound to the monitoring point (audio recordings of intruder's voices have been successfully used in evidence) is both effective and relatively inexpensive.

Always remember that alarm systems need response arrangements. If the site is continually guarded then this can be by local means, otherwise a contract with a security central station is required. The alarm is then transmitted to the central station, usually via telephone line and the contractor identifies the source and contacts the police on an emergency basis. The disadvantages are that:

(a) The police will require a keyholder to be called out as well

(b) Resetting of the alarm system may require a service call to the installation contractor (at silent hours rates)

(c) Excessive false alarms can result in the police withdrawing their response support.

These can be partly diluted by in house remote monitoring by security staff at another site which is continuously manned and commercial call out operated by a security contractor. One must be persuaded by the contractor that response times will be short but police response times are often very poor in any case.

Whilst mentioning remote monitoring (that of an unmanned site by a security central station) we should also consider the slow rate transmission of CCTV pictures. This technology harnesses a site CCTV system to the telephone system and, either by alarm activiation or on demand from the monitoring station, a still picture (renewable every few seconds) of the scene can be inspected for alarm evaluation purposes. This is a very cost effective system if monitoring is carried out by security staff on another site. They can potentially network any number of remote locations thus saving expenditure on manned guarding or contract alarm monitoring, always provided that there is no operational need for the remote site to have continuous human supervision.

Railway Freight Terminals

Railway premises are officially declared prohibited places and are within the jurisdiction of the British Transport Police. However, as mentioned previously, police forces are mainly reactive and little is done in a true security sense. Clearly, the railway is a dangerous place and this does have a deterrent effect, but the freight depots are vast areas and most have a built in perimeter weakness by virtue of the necessary entry and exit of the tracks. The result is that, largely without formal security defences, and generally situated in desolate and criminally hostile areas, railway freight centres are frequented by trespassers, thieves and vandals. Freight trains are relatively safe when on the move but they are often stationary for periods in regular locations, particularly on the approaches to freight depots. In these circumstances, loaded wagons and containers can be attacked and especially if the doors to the latter are unobstructed. Railway container wagons have a capacity of 3 teu (ie 3 twenty foot containers). It is possible to load these with all doors obstructed but this discipline is not always observed. Similarly one 40ft and one 20ft container can be positioned "doors to doors". The impediment to enforcing the discipline comes when weight restrictions apply; the maximum capacity of UK wagons being around 60 tonnes. Therefore, two twenty foot containers, weighing together the majority of the limit, would have to be loaded at either end of the wagon, leaving the doors exposed. Similarly, a very heavy 40ft container may have to be positioned centrally on one wagon.

Generally speaking, the railway cargo in transit is reasonably secure but the problems arise at either end if any period of storage is necessitated. It must be currently accepted in the UK that the physical security of the railway system does have room for improvement but it can be hoped that the establishment of Freight Villages, planned to serve the

Channel Tunnel network, will provide the desired opportunity to put this right. Also, a couple of practical security audit trail points, mentioned elsewhere, are worth repeating here. The railway handling operation can be naturally hard on equipment so it is very important that container seals are of a type which will resist accidental damage. This is also desirable because opportunist thieves thrive on weak strip and light wire seals which are easy to break without tools. The second point arises from the natural vulnerability that has been described. Always ensure that collection agents record their check of seal integrity before accepting custody of the cargo from the railway system.

Haulage Yards

The physical security for hauliers yards can be based on that for our typical cargo depot but, from the freight security viewpoint, there may be scope for slightly less expenditure. If the incidence of loaded vehicles being parked overnight is quite low, and therefore the risk of criminal targetting reduced, good perimeter fencing and gates, combined with a disciplined policy for vehicle and ignition key security, may be adequate. This is always provided that there is an absolute ban on the parking of high value attractive cargo and that sensible precautions such as the use of fifth wheel (King Pin) trailer locks and the positioning of box vans and containers so as to obstruct access to the rear doors are adopted. Given this allowance for dispensation, there can clearly never be any excuse for careless disciplines such as occasional failure to lock the gates or the 'hiding' of keys on vehicles so that early shift drivers can facilitate a quick departure.

It is worth mentioning that many small hauliers do operate from premises which are remote locations and there is a prevalance for regarding a guard dog as the OK solution to crime prevention. There is no doubt of the value of using properly trained dogs to aid security patrol in large enclosed areas; this has been effectively demonstrated by the armed forces, in particular the Royal Air Force Police who protect military airfields. However, the use of these dogs is a specialised skill, has limitations when considering the practicality of wind-scenting techniques in a number of common climatic conditions, and the proper care and supervision of the animals is expensive. If this does not deter the use of guard dogs in most commercial companies, then knowledge of the relevant law should. The UK Guard Dogs Act 1975 requires that:

(a) A person shall not use or permit the use of a guard dog at any premises unless a person (the handler) who is capable of controlling the dog is present on the premises and the dog is under the control of the handler at all times whilst it is being so used except while it is secured so that it is not at liberty to go freely about the premises.

(b) The handler of a guard dog shall keep the dog under his control at all times while it is being used as a guard dog at any premises except

(i) While another handler has control over the dog, or
(ii) While the dog is secured so that it is not at liberty to go freely about the premises.

(c) A person shall not use or permit the use of a guard dog at any premises unless a notice containing a warning that a guard dog is present is clearly exhibited at each entrance to the premises.

In short, there can be no defence for the managing director who is satisfied to secure his yard by locking the gate and leaving a starving Bull Terrier to roam around all night. In any case, a dog cannot raise the alarm in a desolate area and is at the mercy of chemical sprays or indeed firearms.

If the objective is to catch vandals and opportunist thieves then there are better ways which do not run the risk of corporate manslaughter charges or damaging publicity.

I am also very sceptical about the effectiveness of random visits by the proverbial "man and his dog" on a contractual basis. Such operations thrive on volume work which usually results in sparse coverage and in routes and timings being fairly predictable. These days, remotely monitored technical security systems are far superior and less expensive in the long term.

Illus·6   Video Camera Records Drivers Features

Illus·7   Video Monitor Display Driver/Vehicle/Load Details

Chapter 6

Preventing Fraud

PREVENTING FRAUD

A great deal has been written, particularly over the last decade, about maritime fraud. Most of these learned works have concentrated on subjective estimates of the size of losses, case histories and the individual lessons learned from them. Some of the dissertations are virtual text books for would be fraudsters but the real pity is that there have been very few attempts at suggesting practical methods of prevention. The scope of this book does not extend to the type of fraud which involves an international conspiracy to make fantastic financial gains out of deliberately sinking an over-insured ship carrying a non-existant high value cargo. In fact, I would rather talk about deception than fraud. The English law of tort defines fraud as "deceit" which, in simple language, means the advantage taken by a dishonest person over one who demonstrates either a naive lack of awareness or basic carelessness.

At risk of being too simplistic, I might suggest that the best way to avoid becoming the victim of a cargo fraud, is to only deal with the most reputable names in shipping and distribution. I am sure that this is excellent advice but ackowledge that both competitive freight rates and the very nature of international trade, involving remote dealing through multiple agents, make it very difficult to guarantee immunity from fraud.

Bill of Lading Frauds

The bill of lading is the universally utilised document which represents title to the cargo. There are some commodities, such as coffee, which change ownership a number of times as a result of normal trading between the point where they are shipped and the point where they are delivered to the final consignee. It is this remote trading, where a buyer never sees the cargo, only documents, which gives rise to the opportunity for deception. This is usually practised by the seller offering a forgery of an original bill or a genuine bill of lading form, of a reputable shipping company, with the cargo and shipping details forged on to it.

In the first place, most of the forgeries I have seen are fairly poor and simple checks, such as on the texture of the paper, the printing of standard terms and conditions on the rear face of the document and a comparison of authorising signatures (which could be made with the shipping company) would have exposed the deception. Plain photocopies of original bills have been successfully sold and the simple prevention from this type of deception is that such documents are nothing like the real thing. Also, it should be clear that possession of a photocopy is insufficient evidence of title to the original. There are much safer ways of protection against these frauds by the use of security paper, security printing inks and the modern technology of invisible bar-coding. Unfortunately such practise is not yet developed and needs the encouragement and sanction of the financial institutions of the world. However, some shipping companies have added security codes to bills representing vulnerable cargoes and this has been successful in thwarting a number of fraudsters. The case, whereby original bill forms are obtained, either blank or partially prepared, is caused by lack of basic office security effort on the part of the issuing authority. The secure custody and control of blank bills is essential, as are similar precautions with regard to authorising stamps and the printing medium. It is also wise to allocate such responsibility to specific personnel who, having been granted this limited access, should be deterred from collusion with fraudsters because of the potential ease with which they could be connected with the crime. Bills are completed in stages so it is vital to secure the original and numbered copies at all times. In particular, strict control on photocopiers in the office vicinity of where the bills are produced and filed must be maintained. It is a good practise to immobilise these machines after office hours; even simple methods such as the breaking of the mains cable into extension leads and securing the latter under lock and key, can help. While on the subject of photo-copying, there are new developments in producing paper and printing which will deny monochrome copying and these should be seriously considered by commercial departments of shipping companies. The introduction of coloured printing will certainly hinder the fraudster.

Collection Document Frauds

There have been numerous examples of criminals posing as the authorised collection drivers of full loads. This is a particular problem in container operations because of the large number of daily vehicle movements which are normal at terminals, container depots and railway freight centres.

Apart from avoiding the shear negligence demonstrated by some freight forwarders, who leave load collection notes in exposed out trays or even in corridor letter racks outside the office after normal working hours, the answer to this problem is basic document authorisation.

In the first place, documents which authorise the collection of cargo should not be issued too far in advance of the agreed collection time, certainly not more than 24 hours in advance. If a primary haulier is to be used, then the documents should be delivered (in bulk if a complete days work) to the hauliers' office by secure courier. If the courier service is properly recorded in respect of delivery times and signed receipts, then anything that then goes wrong between the primary haulier and any sub-contractor he uses can be proved in liability terms. The haulier must then notify the collection point of the vehicle/driver details allocated to each job. The despatcher at the collection point (who may be a contract security guard) should have the following advance information about the collector.

(a) Name of haulier

(b) Name of driver

(c) HGV registration/index number

(d) Approximate time of collection

(e) Container number to be collected

(f) Destination of load.

These details can be checked against the documents presented by the driver which should, by this time, have some kind of authentication overprinted by the hauliers office. In a case where the orders to the haulier are given at short notice, and either there has not been time to send the collection documents or a sub-conctractor (who may be an owner driver) has been allocated, then the collection documents may have to be issued by the despatcher. In these circumstances, the proper identity checks on the haulier/vehicle/driver which turns up are even more critical. In any event, the despatcher should be able to telephone the primary haulier at any time to double check these details, especially if there is a discrepancy. It is important that the despatcher initiatives this telephone call and not vise-versa when a further check back call would be essential to authenticate the source. Authentication overprinting of these documents, either by haulier on allocation of the work or by despatcher when authorising the cargo release, is best carried out by an automatic stamping machine. These can have sealed mechanisms which produce a stamp indicating serial number, date, time and company logo. If the logo is impressed by a fixed printing plate and coloured ink/ribbon (which can be changed from time to time by confidential arrangement) then security is improved with every mechanism which frustrates forgers.

The issue of the drivers' identity cards (complete with photograph) is another good defence. However, regular despatchers will quickly become familiar with regular drivers and this familiarity is the best form of identity check. It is also another reason why wholesome security guarding contracts should be negotiated (see chapter 2) to encourage a reduction in staff turnover for which that industry is infamous.

These are critical procedures, not only to ensure security of the load and equipment but also to ensure that liability can be accurately attributed if an error is made. Where transaction video recording is implemented, there is a valuable audit check and also a significant deterrent to fraudsters of this type.

Short Loading Claim Frauds

Deliberate short loading claim, or indeed short delivery claim, frauds can be perpetrated if insufficient care is taken by carriers. They can be defeated by rigid driver disciplines on both collection and delivery and call for comprehensive seal recording procedures. These days, except in some commodity areas, there is less use of the weighbridge and this is probably a degradation in general practise. Some control is possible by experience of the sort of volumes which particular cargo quantities consume. Claims for complete non-delivery of cargo are also made and this begs the need for a driver to always obtain proof of delivery in the form of receipts and satisfaction clausing of delivery notes. Some of the investigation techniques described in chapter 7 are of particular use in discovering shortage claims and a company reputation for positive pursuance of such investigations will certainly deter these frauds.

Summary

Fraud will always be featured in the world of trading and good security may not always substitute for the legal loopholes which exist. However, security in the form of tight procedure will considerably reduce exposure to deception which results from a confidence that companies may let standard slips when business is booming. Procedures are dependent on people for their implementation, the human being is fallible and security audit is therefore a continuous necessity.

Chapter 7

Cargo Loss Investigations

GENERAL PRINCIPLES

The bad news is that cargo loss investigations are expensive in financial, manpower and timescale terms. This is because there is no short cut to a comprehensive study of the case involving field enquiries by personnel who understand both the legal techniques of investigation and through transport operations. The enquiries must always be carried out on the assumption that the case could ultimately be heard in a court of law where the defence will ruthlessly examine the extent of investigation and any flaws in the methodology such as ignorance of the UK Police and Criminal Evidence Act (PACE) during the interview of suspects and witnesses.

Two things follow from this. The first, and I make no excuses for being controversial, is that the type of administrative (written and telephonic) enquiries made by some company insurance departments and some loss adjusters are unreliable and largely a waste of effort. Secondly, the need for investigations must be reduced as much as possible.

The good news is that if fundamental preventative security is incorporated into the through transport operation, cargo loss investigations will be few, are simplified and can be very accurate in their findings. Even better, the confidence engendered commercially by such a situation means that compensation claims can be settled quickly in the knowledge that the party responsible for the link of the transport chain where the loss occurred can be successfully held liable and held to account. The benefits are real in terms of claims expediture recovery, enhanced reputation with customers and the incentive to take care by agents and contractors.

An overriding principle is that investigations cannot wait until a formal claim is received, sometimes as much as months after the event. They must be mounted as soon as the complaint is recieved so as to gain the advantage of recent memories and early inspection of pertinent evidence.

Fortunately for investigators, this principle may become more vital due to the requirements of quality accreditation for which most leading European companies are bidding. However, it does mean that, given the overall cost of these investigations, a firm commercial policy must be established for their prompt authorisation. This will probably be based on both the level of financial loss at risk and the relative importance of customer relationships.

Objectives of Investigation

Unlike in criminal investigations the main objective is not to identify and prosecute the thieves, although this may be possible. Incidentally, it usually pays to have a company prosecution policy, with reference to employees, as this can deter the opportunists and result in a high reputation. However, the publicity accrued from the prosecution of employees is not always beneficial as inherrent security weaknesses of routine business functions may be exposed needlessly. A fine balance of judgement is required and each case should be considered in isolation.

The objectives of commercial investigation then are as follows and in order of importance:

    (a)   To recover the loss financially through proof of the liable party and his negligence.

    (b)   To identify weaknesses in procedure and rectify these for the future.

    (c)   To attribute criminal or disciplinary responsibility if possible.

Types of Complaint

There are broadly three types of complaint following loss:

    (a)   Theft of a complete consignment.

    (b)   Theft of a part load (or pilferage).

    (c)   Short delivery.

Short delivery can of course be as a result of pilferage, but also could result from short loading. The theft of a complete consignment may be combined with the loss of the associated equipment such as an HGV, a trailer or a container (or all three). Although the equipment is often recovered later, minus the load, it is quite common for criminals to dispose of HGV's on the open market or broken down into spares. Equipment is frequently never seen again and has been known to be simply destroyed.

Methodology

The following examples of investigation methodology are intended to demonstrate the value of the security plans described in previous chapters and which are assumed to be in place. It is not my intention to guide company directors and line managers how to conduct investigations, other than for them to gain an understanding of how the security audit trail can be used. Furthermore it must be recognised that if managers go beyond preliminary enquiries when major loss complaints are received, they may compromise the professional investigators' chances of constructing a case which is legally sound.

EXAMPLE 1

A consignee reports short (i.e. only part) delivery of a full load compromising of a high value cargo packaged in cartons. He reports that the seal was 'intact' on delivery.

NB 'Seal Intact' is a common expression. It **should** mean that the seal was of the correct (manifested) serial number and that it was closed correctly with no sign of tampering. However, it **could** mean that an apparently closed seal has been removed, to effect unloading, without enough examination to determine that it has, in fact, been tampered with or is not the original.

For the carrier, the enquiry is a defensive one. If the seal was really intact and confirmed as the original by reference to issue records, then he is largely in the clear. However, the removed seal must be recovered for inspection. If there is a further challenge by the claimant or the account is so valuable to the carrier that he feels an obligation to consolidate his innocence, then there are further steps which can be taken as follows:

(a) **Consider Short Loading** Seak liaison with the consignor and evaluate the standard of inventory control, warehouse security and loading disciplines. This can often lead to areas of doubt with regard to how much was loaded. Search for inadvertantly undespatched cartons and observe the demeanour of the consignor.

(a) **Consider Driver Integrity** If (as is often the case) the seal was (wrongly) allowed to be affixed by the driver, then he could have positioned it unclosed. There would then be the opportunity to remove part of the load en route and thereafter close the seal properly. Before jumping to this conclusion, do inspect the vehicle tachograph for route or timing inconsistancies and also consider the illegal disposal possibilities for the particular cargo. For Instance, if it was palleted or the cartons very large, would it have been practical for the collection driver to handle it prior to reporting for the first seal interchange check? Also, if a soft skinned load compartment is involved, were the inherrent weaknesses evident? (see chapter 5).

(c) **Consider Deception of Consignee** Did he declare the shortage immediately on unloading and before the delivery driver left the premises? Was the delivery note so claused and returned to the driver?

(d) **Prove Environmental Vulnerability** Consider each stage of the particular transport chain and ask such questions as:

(i) Did any vehicle involved complete an unaturally extended or uncontrolled journey? (tachograph inspection).

(ii) Did any transit storage location have less than adequate physical security?

(iii)   Were all interchange checks satisfactorily completed?

(iv)   Was the container stowed in an inaccessible bay position on the ship?

The answer to each of the above questions will serve to indicate whether or not maximum care was taken.

EXAMPLE 2

A consignee reports short delivery. The seal removed at the time of unloading is produced and is not the same as that at loading.

This is a real test of the seal audit trail which is the only weapon in the armoury capable of determining the point of loss. If the seal is rogue, then we are looking for the interchange check which recorded a change of serial number. It would be the same procedure for an authorised seal with incorrect serial number, but this time the audit trail may reveal a legitimate reason for re-sealing during transit. Examples of these are for customs inspection or port health examination. However, I must comment that pilferage is not unknown in conjunction with these events.

If examination of the audit trail reveals an unexplained seal change, then the investigation has reached the point of concentrated field enquiry. Who conducts the enquiry is a matter of jurisdiction but it will be very important that legal rules of procedure (e.g. PACE) are complied with.

EXAMPLE 3

A container is called forward for delivery from the last interchange point in the through transport chain. The delivery driver reports to collect the container but it cannot be located. It is then reported as missing, believed stolen.

FCL theft is the nightmare of the through transport world. Often there will be very clear evidence of theft at the outset, such as record of the container being collected a short time earlier than the legitimate driver's arrival. However, if this is not the case, the investigation may develop as follows:

(a)   **Establish Proof of Delivery (POD)** First prove that the container actually arrived at the collection point. This will be done by the examination of documents and, most likely, computer records. At locations like terminals and railfreight depots, there should be equipment interchange reports and stock position certificates. If this information is data based then, at large area locations, be wary of the ''garbage in-garbage out'' syndrome; whilst there is no argument against the stock control efficiency provided by computers, there does need to be reconcilliations based on physical inspection (perhaps incorporated within silent hours security patrols) when loaded containers are stored for extended periods. Indeed criminals, in collusion with terminal staff, have been known to amend a stock control data base from time to time to give the illusion of continuing custody of a particular container which has been stolen from the site days or weeks earlier.

(b)   **Examine Release Records** If there is documentary evidence of previous collection then this should be studied for signs of forging etc. Should a video recorded release system be available, then the tape must be seized and immediately subjected to evidence continuity procedures and examination for clues to vehicle and driver identity. All interviews of staff must be in accordance with PACE and, if an error has been made by the releasing authorities (possibly a security guard) the appropriate agency must be held formally liable. The police may need to be involved at this point.

EXAMPLE 4

Refridgerated cargo is reported short delivered This warrants a brief mention because of the availability of temperature maintained records which may show a variation caused by opening the container doors at a particular point.

Obviously, there will be various forms of investigation progress; every case is different. However, the examples given do demonstrate the many advantages of comprehensive security controls within the cargo handling system.

Covert Investigations

It is sometimes necessary to conduct covert investigations to solve a series of apparently unexplained losses. Often this results from the approach by a customer to a carrier reporting a number of relatively minor losses, which, in isolation, may have been regarded as inventory control errors.

A pre-requisite for such an investigation is to agree between concerned parties that the enquiries will not be overtly conducted for fear that any illicit activities will be suspended until the "hue and cry" dies down. It follows that only a minimum number of persons are made aware of investigation, typically very senior managers, any trusted key personnel who will be needed to facilitate the enquiry and the investigators themselves.

The first step however, is an administrative collation of all the facts known about previous incidents e.g. Dates, times, locations, routes, personalities. In some very complicated cases, there is advantage in using a computer for this collation and commercial software is available for this purpose. The objective is to establish commonalities between the incidents which will give rise to a concentrated enquiry into the activities at a particular location or of particular individuals. Only then can a covert field investigation be mounted. Sufficient justification for this will need to be firmly ratified because such a commitment is expensive, not easily terminated at short notice and can be hazardous in terms of both investigators' personal safety and industrial relations. The operation necessary usually involves covert surveillance using either trained personnel or special equipment and can sometimes benefit by the injection of a "mole" (an investigator skilled in transport and distribution operations) into a workforce. This is a very specialised area but it is a realistic option in many cases and some outstanding results have been obtained.

Conclusion

In summary, there will always be the need for some investigations but the aim must be for the need to be minimal. Commercial security is about loss prevention and the correct balance is for the preventative effort to monopolise the time of security managers. If the reverse is true in your company, then it is time to re-examine your security policy.

GLOSSARY OF TERMS

Accompanied Load — TIR operation where a dedicated driver hauls the load door to door.

Assignment Instructions — The details of work to be performed within a guarding contract.

Bay plan — Plan of a containership showing the loading position of each container.

Bill of Lading — A single shipping document which represents title to a cargo and also records receipt of the goods and evidence of carriage contract.

Box — Colloquial term for "container".

Box-van — HGV or trailer with fixed hard-skinned load compartment.

C C D — Charged Coupled Device, solid state (CCTV camera).

CCTV — Closed circuit television.

Carrier — The person contracted to carry the goods.

Consignee — The person accepting final delivery of the goods.

Consignor — The person despatching the goods.

Consolidation — The accumulation of cargo from different sources for transportation as one load.

Container — Stand alone load compartment used in through transport incorporating intermodal transit.

Curtain Sider — HGV, trailer load compartment or container with soft-skinned side walls.

FCL — Full Container Load (single consignment).

Feeder Vessel — Small (container) ship used to disperse cargo unloaded from deep sea (container) ship over local sea routes.

Fifth wheel lock — Device used to lock the coupling of an articulated trailer and prevent unauthorised movement of the trailer.

Guarding Contractor — Company supplying security guards.

HGV — Heavy Goods Vehicle.

ICD — Inland Clearance Depot. Customs authorised freight depot to where goods may be transported swiftly from the port, uncleared, for clearance close to the point of delivery.

I D S — Intruder Detection System.

Interchange point — The point in a through transport chain where the physical custody of the cargo changes.

King Pin Lock — Fifth wheel lock.

LCL — Less than a full container load (a number of consignments in one container).

Manifest — The complete detailed list of a ships cargo.

Multi-drop — Transit operation whereby a vehicle is unloaded in parts at various locations on a journey.

Open top — Container with soft skinned roof to allow for top loading and 'overheight' cargo.

P.A.C.E. — (UK) Police and Criminal Evidence Act 1984. Includes rules for investigation procedure.

P O D — Proof of Delivery.

P T Z — Pan, Tilt, Zoom; expression used to describe a fully functional (remote control) CCTV camera.

Railfreight Terminal	—	Railway goods yard where containerised cargo is transferred between rail and road transport.
REEFER	—	Refridgerated (container) Load Compartment.
Roll-on/Roll-off	—	A specialised cargo ship or ferry designed to carry HGV's or road trailers.
Seal Audit Trail	—	Complete transit record of a uniquely coded security seal.
Security Central Station	—	Control room where security alarm activations are monitored and response arranged.
Security seal	—	A seal which indicates tampering and cannot be reinstated in a sealed condition after removal.
Shipper	—	The person/Company/Agent who provides the goods for despatch and whose name appears on the consignment note as the party contracting with the carrier for the carriage of goods.
Stack	—	Containers can be stacked on top of each other for storage purposes on land or in transit on a ship.
Stowaway	—	Person who secretly conceals himself on a ship to gain free passage.
Strip	—	Unload a container.
Stuff	—	Load a container.
TEU	—	Twenty foot Equivalent Unit, expression used to quantify the container carrying capacity (eg of a ship).
T.I.R.	—	(Transport International Routier), International road haulage transit operation.
Taut Liner	—	Tilt.
Terminal	—	Facility for the berthing of ships and handling of cargo within a sea port.
Through Transport	—	The complete operation involved in the transit of goods from "door to door".
Tilt	—	Soft-skinned load compartment.
Transhipment Port	—	Port where cargo is transferred between ships for further onward transit by sea.

INDEX